D0686195

DIVINE PRESENCE AND
COMMUNITY

INTERNATIONAL THEOLOGICAL COMMENTARY

Fredrick Carlson Holmgren and George A. F. Knight
General Editors

Volumes now available

DIVINE PRESENCE AND COMMUNITY

A Commentary on the Book of

Leviticus

FRANK H. GORMAN, JR.

WM. B. EERDMANS PUBLISHING CO., GRAND RAPIDS

THE HANDSEL PRESS LTD, EDINBURGH

© 1997 Wm. B. Eerdmans Publishing Company
First published 1997 by Wm. B. Eerdmans Publishing Company,
255 Jefferson Ave. S.E., Grand Rapids, Michigan 49503
and
The Handsel Press Limited
The Stables, Carberry, EH21 8PY, Scotland

00 99 98 97 96 95   7 6 5 4 3 2 1

Library of Congress Cataloging-in-Publication Data

Gorman, Frank H.
Divine presence and community: a commentary on the Book of Leviticus /
Frank Gorman, Jr.
p.   cm.   — (International theological commentary)
Includes bibliographical references.
ISBN 0-8028-0110-2 (pbk.: alk. paper)
1. Bible. O.T. Leviticus — Commentary.
I. Title. II. Series.
BS1255.3.G67 1997
222′.1306 — dc21   97-25267
CIP

Handsel Press ISBN 1 871828 40 6

CONTENTS

ABBREVIATIONS

JB	Jerusalem Bible
KJV	King James (or Authorized) Version
LXX	Septuagint
NAB	New American Bible
NEB	New English Bible
NIV	New International Version
NJPS	New Jewish Publication Society version
NRSV	New Revised Standard Version
RSV	Revised Standard Version
REB	Revised English Bible
TEV	Today's English Version

EDITORS' PREFACE

The Old Testament alive in the Church: this is the goal of the *International Theological Commentary*. Arising out of changing, unsettled times, this Scripture speaks with an authentic voice to our own troubled world. It witnesses to God's ongoing purpose and to God's caring presence in the universe without ignoring those experiences of life that cause one to question God's existence and love. This commentary series is written by front-rank scholars who treasure the life of faith.

Addressed to ministers and Christian educators, the *International Theological Commentary* moves beyond the usual critical-historical approach to the Bible and offers a *theological* interpretation of the Hebrew text. Thus, engaging larger textual units of the biblical writings, the authors of these volumes assist the reader in the appreciation of the theology underlying the text as well as its place in the thought of the Hebrew Scriptures. But more, since the Bible is the book of the believing community, its text has acquired ever more meaning through an ongoing interpretation. This growth of interpretation may be found both within the Bible itself and in the continuing scholarship of the Church.

Contributors to the *International Theological Commentary* are Christians — persons who affirm the witness of the New Testament concerning Jesus Christ. For Christians, the Bible is *one* Scripture containing the Old and New Testaments. For this reason, a commentary on the Old Testament may not ignore the second part of the canon, namely, the New Testament.

Since its beginning, the Church has recognized a special relationship between the two Testaments. But the precise character of this bond has been difficult to define. Thousands of books and

vii

articles have discussed the issue. The diversity of views represented in these publications makes us aware that the Church is not of one mind in expressing the "how" of this relationship. The authors of this commentary share a developing consensus that any serious explanation of the Old Testament's relationship to the New will uphold the integrity of the Old Testament. Even though Christianity is rooted in the soil of the Hebrew Scriptures, the biblical interpreter must take care lest he or she "christianize" these Scriptures.

Authors writing in this commentary will, no doubt, hold varied views concerning *how* the Old Testament relates to the New. No attempt has been made to dictate one viewpoint in this matter. With the whole Church, we are convinced that the relationship between the two Testaments is real and substantial. But we recognize also the diversity of opinions among Christian scholars when they attempt to articulate fully the nature of this relationship.

In addition to the Christian Church, there exists another people for whom the Old Testament is important, namely, the Jewish community. Both Jews and Christians claim the Hebrew Bible as Scripture. Jews believe that the basic teachings of this Scripture point toward, and are developed by, the Talmud, which assumed its present form about 500 C.E. On the other hand, Christians hold that the Old Testament finds its fulfillment in the New Testament. The Hebrew Bible, therefore, belongs to both the Church and the Synagogue.

Recent studies have demonstrated how profoundly early Christianity reflects a Jewish character. This fact is not surprising because the Christian movement arose out of the context of first-century Judaism. Further, Jesus himself was Jewish, as were the first Christians. It is to be expected, therefore, that Jewish and Christian interpretations of the Hebrew Bible will reveal similarities *and* disparities. Such is the case. The authors of the *International Theological Commentary* will refer to the various Jewish traditions that they consider important for an appreciation of the Old Testament text. Such references will enrich our understanding of certain biblical passages and, as an extra gift, offer us insight into the relationship of Judaism to early Christianity.

An important second aspect of the present series is its *international* character. In the past, Western church leaders were considered to be *the* leaders of the Church — at least by those living in the West! The theology and biblical exegesis done by these scholars dominated the thinking of the Church. Most commentaries were produced in the Western world and reflected the lifestyle, needs, and thoughts of its civilization. But the Christian Church is a worldwide community. People who belong to this universal Church reflect differing thoughts, needs, and lifestyles.

Today the fastest growing churches in the world are to be found, not in the West, but in Africa, Indonesia, South America, Korea, Taiwan, and elsewhere. By the end of this century, Christians in these areas will outnumber those who live in the West. In our age, especially, a commentary on the Bible must transcend the parochialism of Western civilization and be sensitive to issues that are the special problems of persons who live outside of the "Christian" West, issues such as race relations, personal survival and fulfillment, liberation, revolution, famine, tyranny, disease, war, the poor, and religion and state. Inspired of God, the authors of the Old Testament knew what life is like on the edge of existence. They addressed themselves to everyday people who often faced more than everyday problems. Refusing to limit God to the "spiritual," they portrayed God as one who heard and knew the cries of people in pain (see Exod. 3:7-8). The contributors to the *International Theological Commentary* are persons who prize the writings of these biblical authors as a word of life to our world today. They read the Hebrew Scriptures in the twin contexts of ancient Israel and our modern day.

The scholars selected as contributors underscore the international aspect of the series. Representing very different geographical, ideological, and ecclesiastical backgrounds, they come from more than seventeen countries. Besides scholars from such traditional countries as England, Scotland, France, Italy, Switzerland, Canada, New Zealand, Australia, South Africa, and the United States, contributors from the following places are included: Israel, Indonesia, India, Thailand, Singapore, Taiwan, and countries of Eastern Europe. Such diversity makes for richness of thought. Christian scholars living in Buddhist, Muslim, or Socialist lands may be able to offer the World Church insights into the biblical message — insights to which the scholarship of the West could be blind.

The proclamation of the biblical message is the focal concern of the *International Theological Commentary*. Generally speaking, the authors of these commentaries value the historical-critical studies of past scholars, but they are convinced that these studies by themselves are not enough. The Bible is more than an object of critical study; it is the revelation of God. In the written Word, God has disclosed himself and his will to humankind. Our authors see themselves as servants of the Word which, when rightly received, brings *shalom* to both the individual and the community.

— GEORGE A. F. KNIGHT
— FREDRICK CARLSON HOLMGREN

AUTHOR'S PREFACE

I have attempted to write a theological commentary on the book of Leviticus that seeks to speak a word of life to the church. What is "theological" in Leviticus and, probably more importantly, how might one find a word of "life" in this book? I have found the answer to both questions in recognizing that the book must be read in the context of a concrete image: the divine presence dwelling in the midst of the Israelite community. Leviticus explores some of the dynamics of what it means for the community to live in the presence of the holy God. At the heart of this exploration is a focus on the ways in which the community enacts holiness. Both the enactment of holiness and the Yahweh-Israel relationship are theologically located in the story of Israel's journey to freedom.

I am especially grateful to John Hayes for his ongoing support of my work on Leviticus and ritual. Fredrick Holmgren, George A. F. Knight, and Allen Myers demonstrated patience and offered encouragement during the writing process. I extend a special word of thanks to Fredrick Holmgren for his support and kindness as the project drew to a close. Finally, I must thank my spouse Kimberly for her encouragement and patience. She has listened as I have struggled to understand the relationship between enactment and theology, and she has provided insightful comments on a number of issues relating to enactment and human existence.

I dedicate the book to my children, Melissa and Zachary, who have taught me in a variety of unexpected ways a great deal about love, integrity, enactment, and community.

— FRANK H. GORMAN, JR.
June 1997

xi

INTRODUCTION

TITLE AND OVERVIEW

Leviticus is the third book of the Bible and is located at the center of the Pentateuch. Its Hebrew title is the first word of the book, *wayyiqra'*, "and he called." The English "Leviticus" is taken from the Latin Vulgate translation, which is based on the Septuagint, the Greek translation. This title reflects the book's focus on matters associated with the levitical priesthood. Leviticus, however, is also important for laypersons. It constitutes a significant effort to address the question of Israelite identity. What does it mean to be the people of God, redeemed from slavery, called to be holy, with Yahweh in the midst of the community? It is a book of and about community, and what it means to be a community confronted daily with the promise and warning of divine presence.

The book covers a variety of subjects and issues: several chapters describe or prescribe ritual activities (e.g., 1–7; 8–9; 16); others give instructions regarding what is pure and impure for a range of issues (e.g., 11–15); and several texts focus on what might be termed ethical matters (e.g., 18–26). Leviticus itself does not make such categorical (generic) distinctions. It understands ritual, instructions on what is pure and impure, and ethics to be of the same cloth. Together they provide a means for the individual and the community to enact life in the context of the divine presence. Ritual matters, ethical issues, and rulings on purity are all part of Yahweh's words to the community, and they carry equal weight and significance.

1

AUTHORSHIP AND DATE

The materials in Leviticus belong to the priestly traditions of the Pentateuch. Generally, these traditions are located in the Babylonian Exile, in the 6th cent. B.C.E.. Several recent studies, however, locate the cultic materials in an earlier period (see Milgrom 1991, 13-35; Knohl 1995, 199-224). An exilic date for the writing of these traditions does not necessarily mean that the practices envisioned in the texts were of exilic origin. Cultic practices similar to the ones in Leviticus are found elsewhere in the ancient Near East and arose in Israel at an early date. As Israel reflected on the nature of its existence and identity in changing historical situations, it adapted its traditions, practices, and ritual life. The community's ritual practices would reflect the historical contexts in which they were enacted in the same way that texts reflect the historical situations in which they were written.

In the present work, "the priestly traditions" refer to pentateuchal texts that share common language, style, thematics, and content; they reflect the work of "the priestly traditionists." These traditions, which give voice to the ritual, ethical, social, and religious reflection undertaken by priestly groups throughout Israel's history, were collected, written down, and placed in the larger pentateuchal narrative in the exilic period. They reflect the priestly struggle to understand the meaning of Israel's existence and to provide a means for enacting that existence in the context of the Israelite community.

STRUCTURE AND CONTENT

The structure of the book of Leviticus is fairly simple.
  I. Instructions for Offerings and Sacrifices (1–7)
      A. Series one (1:1–6:7 [Heb. 5:26])
      B. Series two (6:8 [Heb. 6:1]–7:38)
  II. Ordination, Founding, and Tragedy (8–10)
      A. The ordination of the priesthood (8)
      B. The founding of the tabernacle cult (9)
      C. The strange fire of Nadab and Abihu (10)

The book opens with two series of instructions regarding sacrifices and offerings (1:1–6:7 [Heb. 1:1–5:26] and 6:8 [Heb. 6:1]–7:38). These chapters provide foundational instructions for the more complex rituals that follow. Chapter 8 narrates the ordination ritual for priests, and ch. 9 narrates the priestly inauguration of the tabernacle cult. On the day of the inauguration, Nadab and Abihu, two of Aaron's sons, offer "strange fire" before Yahweh and are killed (ch. 10).

Several chapters follow that provide instructions for the identification of what is pure and impure: clean and unclean foods (11); impurity and purification associated with childbirth (12); skin diseases and fungal growths (13–14); and bodily discharges (15). These instructions provide a map for the priestly work of separating the clean from the unclean (10:10-11). Leviticus 16 prescribes the enactment of the annual ritual of purification.

Leviticus 17–26, commonly called "the holiness code," contain a variety of genres and themes that focus on the divine call for the community to be holy. The call for holiness weaves together ritual and ethical issues and concerns about purity as it seeks to define the nature of the holy community as that community enacts its life in the presence of Yahweh. The book closes with a series of miscellaneous instructions regarding the maintenance of the sanctuary (ch. 27).

Three significant redactional features of the book must be noted. First, the book emphasizes that the instructions are of divine origin. These are the words of Yahweh for the community. Second, the book emphasizes that things were done "just as Yahweh had commanded" (8:4, 9, 13, 17, 21, 29, 36; 9:7, 21; 16:34; 24:23). This formula is found throughout the priestly traditions and emphasizes that Israel faithfully enacted the instructions of Yahweh (see Blenkinsopp 1976). Third, there are several summary passages in Leviticus (7:37-38; 11:46-47; 13:59; 14:54-57; 15:32-33; 26:46; 27:34). Many of these were, in all probability, already found at the end of the unit of material with which they are now associated. They conclude discussions and mark shifts in content.

THE PENTATEUCHAL CONTEXT

Any adequate theological interpretation of Leviticus must recognize its location within the larger pentateuchal context. Leviticus is part of the story of Israel's origins, experience, and existence (see Sanders 1972, 1-53; 1987, 9-60). The story opens with the creation of the world and human beings (Gen. 1–2) and closes with the death of Moses (Deut. 34). Leviticus is at the center of this story.

Leviticus looks back to four specific moments. First, these instructions are located within the context of creation theology (especially Gen. 1:1–2:4a). God constructs the very good order of creation out of chaos in a seven-day process that reflects both ritual and liturgical characteristics (Gorman 1993, 50-54). The instructions of Leviticus are provided as a means of maintaining and, when necessary, restoring the very good order of creation.

Second, the instructions draw on the promise and covenant that God made with the ancestors (especially Gen. 17). This covenant included the promise of many descendants (a reflection of the divine blessing in creation [Gen. 1:28]), who would inherit a land and enter into a distinctive relationship with God. Leviticus provides instructions for how the people are to live in the context of the divine promises.

Third, the instructions recall the Exodus from Egypt, God's act of redemption on behalf of the Israelites. Yahweh brought Israel out of Egypt in order to dwell in their midst (Exod. 29:43-46). The Exodus becomes part of God's enactment of the covenant promises — I will be their God and they will be my people — as well as one way in which Yahweh makes a claim on the people. The instructions of Leviticus provide a means for the community to respond to Yahweh's redemptive activity.

4

Fourth, the Sinai covenant provides context for the instructions of Leviticus. The instructions then provide one means for manifesting the life of the covenant community in the presence of Yahweh, a means for enacting the covenant relationship.

Thus, the instructions of Leviticus are located within the narrative *and* theological contexts of creation, promise, redemption, and covenant. Both ritual and social enactment are means of actualizing and "bodying forth" the story. The divine presence dwells in the midst of the community (see Newing 1981; 1985; Gorman 1990, 39-60). The ritual and social enactments envisioned and called for in Leviticus are ways of actualizing this particular vision of reality within the context of the flesh-and-blood world of a living community.

THEOLOGY AND RITUAL IN LEVITICUS

To many, the production of a theological commentary on the book of Leviticus might seem impossible: What does ritual have to do with theology? This view reflects a bias against ritual, a bias found in Protestantism and Western Enlightenment thought, and a privileging of "discursive" theology (see Gorman 1994, 14-26). It values thinking over enacting (see Bell 1992, 13-66), mind over body. What is theological in relation to Leviticus and its rituals?

First, the theology of Leviticus must be located within the category of human enactment. Human beings not only "think" their lives; they also enact them. Enactment is not simply the attempt to act out what one believes, although it can be this. It is also a means in, by, and through which human beings discover what they believe — about the self, others, the world, and God. Thus, enactment is a way of "knowing" (Grimes 1992; Grosz 1993; Jennings 1982).

Second, enactment is not only a matter of knowledge and reflection; it also has to do with the location of the self and/or community. Humans locate themselves in the world through enactment, standing forth, the foundational gesture. Locative enactment requires an affirmation of the value of activity as well as an acceptance of the bodied nature of human existence.

Humans "take a stand" in the world as bodied beings who live out and experience themselves, others, and the world, in, by, and through their bodies.

Third, the category of enactment is capable of holding together ritual activity and social activity. Too often, theological discourse has emphasized the importance of social enactment without locating it within the larger context of human enactment. Both ritual and social situations provide contexts for the active engagement of the self with the world, others, and God. Rather than creating a sharp dichotomy between ritual practice and social practice, it is better to recognize that both are means in, by, and through which individuals and communities "act out" their identity.

Fourth, this suggests that ritual (and social enactment as well!) should be discussed in the context of performance. Performance suggests an acting out for an audience, which in turn reflects on the enactment that is being either observed or, in some cases, participated in. Performance is an important category for rituals enacted before the eyes of the community (e.g., chs. 8, 9, 16). The ritual performance constructs a context for individual and community identity through participation and reflection.

Fifth, for the priestly traditionists, ritual is a means of theological enactment and reflection. It is a means of "doing theology" or of "theological enactment." As such, it is not only a means of acting on one's beliefs but also a means of discovering one's beliefs. It is a way of participating in world construction and world maintenance. Ritual is a means of engaging the self, the community, the world, and God. The meaning of ritual is found in the enactment of the ritual itself.

A "theological" commentary on the rituals of Leviticus, then, must attempt to understand the world of ritual — the world within which ritual takes place and the world that is, in part, constituted in, by, and through the rituals. It must not attempt to explain away the actions only in terms of their cognitive meanings. Ritual commentary must seek to recognize ritual enactments and ritual performances for what they are — attempts to locate the self and the community within the world. It is clear, however, that the priestly traditions have a great deal to say about God, the world, the community, and the self, and it is clear that they say these things in conjunction with what they have to say about ritual. A theological commentary on Leviticus must seek to locate itself within both the ritual world and the theological world of the priestly traditionists. Theological reflections on priestly rituals will focus on the ways in which rituals function to constitute and locate the self and the community in relation to God, the world of creation, and the community.

A few final notes regarding some of the assumptions that are operative in this work. First, there is no effort to find a universal or general meaning for each type of sacrifice and offering. Their precise meaning or function will depend on the context within which they are presented (Anderson 1992). Second, the ritual instructions are understood to provide frameworks for enactment and guidelines for activity. Rather than seeing them as rigid rules that must be followed with absolute precision, they will be viewed as guides that allow for personal nuancing and configuring. Third, the comments recognize that the priestly ritual traditions and the priestly narrative traditions are interconnected. Rituals can help interpret narratives, and narratives can help interpret rituals. Fourth, priestly ritual has to do with human life and existence, flesh and blood existence, within the context of community. Ritual processes provide occasions for enacting the self within the context of a community that exists in the presence of God.

RITUAL PROCESSES IN THE PRIESTLY TRADITIONS

The priestly traditions contain a wide variety of ritual processes. At one end of the spectrum are rituals of purification that require only that a person wash herself or himself and wait until evening in order to be clean (e.g., Lev. 11:39-40). At the other end are complex rituals of purification that require multiple washings, several sacrifices, and obeisance for seven or eight days (e.g., 8; 14:1-20). In all cases, it is important to recognize that what is crucial is the entire ritual *process*.

Three basic types of ritual processes are found in the priestly traditions: rituals of founding, rituals of maintenance, and rituals of restoration (Gorman 1993, 48-50; Nelson 1993, 55-59). *Ritu-*

als of founding have as their model the ritual construction of the cosmos by God in Gen. 1:1–2:4a. These rituals function to bring into being that which did not exist before the enactment of the ritual. Thus, Exod. 40:16-33 narrates the ritual construction of sacred space, while Lev. 8–9 narrates the creation of sacred status for the priests and the tabernacle. *Rituals of maintenance* function to maintain the order that has already been created. This process reflects the view that human beings are called upon to maintain the very good order of creation that was brought into being by God. Examples of rituals of maintenance are the observance of the sabbath (Exod. 31:12-17), the regular, daily burnt offerings (Exod. 29:38-46), the annual day of purification (Lev. 16), and the ritual times specified in Num. 28–29. Finally, *rituals of restoration* function to restore the "normative" (created) state when it has been disrupted or violated by sin or impurity. So, for example, the purification sacrifices function, in part, to cleanse the holy place of impurity (Lev. 4), and the ritual for the person recovered from a skin disease functions to restore that person to society (Lev. 14:1-20).

These ritual types are not presented in an effort to impose rigid structures on ritual processes. They attempt to provide some interpretive order to the rituals described and prescribed in these texts. Ritual is the enactment and performance of dynamic processes; it is not a rigid adherence to rules. Ritual processes constitute part of the dynamics of Israelite life. They reflect the joys, sorrows, fears, and hopes of the Israelites as they are actually experienced and lived. Leviticus, then, has to do with a theology of lived experience within the community of God.

The Number Seven in the Priestly Traditions

The number seven plays a significant role in a series of priestly texts (Gorman 1990, 45-52). The priestly traditions open with a seven-day process of world construction (Gen. 1:1–2:4a). Emphasis is placed on the movement from chaos (*tohu wabohu*, v. 2) to order; seven days are required to complete the process. Creation thus provides a paradigm for the temporal process required to effect passage from one state to another.

"Creation" continues when, in Exod. 25–31, Yahweh gives instructions for the construction of the tabernacle in seven speeches (see Blenkinsopp 1976; Kearney 1977; Fishbane 1979, 11-13). The seven speeches are marked by the phrase, "and Yahweh said to Moses" (25:1; 30:11, 17, 22, 34; 31:1, 12). The plan of the tabernacle is "revealed" by Yahweh and reflects the ongoing process of creation. Moses erects the tabernacle in seven acts (Exod. 40:17-33; note the phrase "just as Yahweh commanded him" in vv. 19, 21, 23, 25, 27, 29, 32). The construction of the tabernacle continues the creative activity of Yahweh in constructing the cosmos. It continues the "process" of creation.

Following the construction of the tabernacle, instructions for activity appropriate to holy space are provided (Lev. 1–7). These instructions are themselves an extension of the creative "speech" of Yahweh.

Finally, the ordination of the priesthood is constructed around seven ritual moments (Lev. 8:4, 9, 13, 17, 21, 29, 36, marked by the phrase that Moses did "just as Yahweh commanded him"). The ritual locates the priests within holy space. Through the repeated use of seven speeches and seven acts, the ongoing process of creation is seen to extend from the founding of the cosmos to the founding of the tabernacle cult. Cult is an extension of cosmos; ritual enacts creation.

Ritual practices and processes also employ the number seven. First, in several rituals the priest sprinkles either blood or oil seven times (e.g., blood in Lev. 4:6, 17; 14:7; 16:14, 19; Num. 19:4; oil in Lev. 8:11; 14:16, 27). The purpose of the sprinkling varies from ritual to ritual (purification in Lev. 16:14, 19; preparation in 14:16; consecration in 8:11).

Second, a person can become unclean for seven days. For example, a woman is unclean for seven days when she gives birth to a male child (12:2) or when she is menstruating (15:19). A man who has sexual intercourse with a menstruating woman (15:24), as well as a person who comes into contact with a corpse (Num. 19:11), is unclean for seven days. In these examples, the seven days provide a temporal period for impurity and indicate its severity.

Seven-day rituals effect major ritual passage. For example, a person who has recovered from a skin disease undertakes a ritual process that includes a seven-day period (Lev. 14:1-20). In addition, the ordination ritual for the priesthood requires seven days (Exod. 29:35; Lev. 8:33, 35). It functions to move the priests from lay status to an ordained and institutionalized status.

In the priestly construction of the sacred year (Lev. 23; Num. 28–29), seven-day periods play a key role. The seventh day of the week is to be observed and set apart (Lev. 23:3). Two seven-day festivals are observed: "unleavened bread" in the first month (vv. 4-8) and "booths" in the seventh month (vv. 33-36, 39-43). In addition, seven "holy days" are marked out (vv. 7, 8, 21, 24, 27, 35, 36). The year is given a sacred rhythm through the observance of holy days and holy times marked by the number seven.

Related to this is the call for the observance of a Sabbatical Year for the land (Lev. 25:1-7). This takes place in the seventh year. The text also calls for the observance of the Jubilee Year. This is a year of release and redemption (vv. 8-55) and is determined by counting off seven weeks of years (v. 8). The rhythm and movement of the week, the year, and the years are marked out, in part, through the number seven.

Thus, in the priestly traditions seven indicates movement and passage. This emphasizes that ritual processes are concerned with movement, passage, restoration, construction, and reconstruction. They effect changes in status: from impurity to purity (14:1-20); from common to holy (8:1-36); from chaos to order (16:1-34).

ELEMENTS OF PRIESTLY THEOLOGY

Divine Presence

At the heart of priestly theology is the belief that Yahweh dwells in the midst of the Israelite community and participates in its story. Indeed, this story is mutually shared and enacted by Yahweh and Israel. The holy God dwelling in the midst of the holy community is a constitutive image of Israel's identity.

This image is concretely envisioned in the tabernacle, the large tent at the center of the community. Yahweh dwells in the holy of holies, the inner sanctum of the tent, above the ark of the covenant. Newing has argued that the Hexateuch reflects a chiastic structure, with the image of the divine presence (Exod. 33) at its center (1981). The divine presence dwelling in the holy place is at the heart of the priestly story and priestly theology. The ritual enactments focus on the divine presence, and the community is to reflect the holiness of the God in its midst. The priestly redaction of Exod. 19–Lev. 16 focuses on the presence of Yahweh and the construction and maintenance of holy space (Gorman 1990, 45-52). The holy place must remain both holy *and* clean. The priestly traditions believe that sin generates impurity (see Milgrom 1991, 253-92). In addition, common experiences may generate impurity (e.g., childbirth, sexual intercourse, and abnormal bodily discharges). Impurity is attracted to and pollutes the tabernacle, violating and disrupting the sacred order. Failure to purify ritually the sacred space might result in Yahweh's departure, which would be catastrophic for Israel.

The Tabernacle

The tabernacle area (see Milgrom 1991, 135) is marked out by a large rectangular tent 50 cubits wide and 100 cubits long (approximately 75 feet by 150 feet) oriented along an east-to-west axis with the entrance facing east. Entering this structure from the east, one is in the outer courtyard. For convenience, the courtyard may be divided into two parts, each measuring 50 cubits by 50 cubits. At the center of the eastern square of the courtyard is the altar of burnt offerings, and approximately 15 cubits beyond the altar, moving along an east-to-west line, is the laver of water for ritual washing. The outer altar of burnt offerings is the place to which the Israelites bring and present their sacrifices and offerings. Just beyond the laver is the entrance to the tent, the holy dwelling place of Yahweh. It too is rectangular, 10 cubits wide and 30 cubits long (approximately 15 feet by 45 feet), and consists of two rooms. The outer room, measuring 10 cubits by 20 cubits (approximately 15 feet by 30 feet), contains the table for the bread, the golden candle holder, and the altar of incense. The inner room, the holy of holies, is a square, 10 cubits by 10 cubits (approximately 15 feet by 15 feet), which houses the ark of the covenant. The divine presence is associated specifically with the ark.

Exod. 40:16-38 narrates that when Moses erected the tabernacle, the divine glory filled it in the sight of all the people. The significant number of verbal parallels between Exod. 40:34-38 and Exod. 24:15-18, the description of the glory of Yahweh on Mt. Sinai, indicates that the divine glory seen initially on the mountain has now taken up residence in the tent. The presence of Yahweh makes the tent "holy" (Exod. 29:43-44). At the same time, however, Lev. 8 states that the holiness of the sacred area is also ritually established (see v. 10). The holiness of the tabernacle is created both by the presence of Yahweh *and* the ritual act of "making holy." Holiness is a shared construct!

Four texts will demonstrate the significance of the tabernacle as a theological construct (see Gorman 1993, 54-59). In *Exod. 25:1-9,* Yahweh calls for the people to contribute materials for the construction of the tabernacle. This is to be the divine dwelling place (v. 8).

Exodus 29:44-46 locates the divine presence within the narrative and theological context of the Exodus story. The Exodus from Egypt took place in order that Yahweh might dwell in the midst of the people of Israel (cf. Exod. 6:2-8). The tabernacle is an expression of the future that God anticipates in redeeming Israel from the slavery and oppression of Egypt. This text also recalls the promise made to the ancestors (Gen. 17:8: "I will be their God"). Thus, the tabernacle is a partial but concrete actualization of the ancestral promise, and as the divine dwelling place it is a manifestation of the promise actualized and redemption realized.

Exodus 25:10-22 provides the instructions for the construction of the ark of the covenant. It is a small rectangular box — 1.5 cubits wide, 2.5 cubits long, and 1.5 cubits deep (approximately 2.25 feet by 3.75 feet by 2.25 feet) — placed within the holy of holies. It was made of acacia wood overlaid with gold. The tablets containing the words of the covenant were placed inside the ark, and the "seat of expiation" was placed on top of the ark and was decorated with cherubim. The concluding statement (v. 22) associates the divine presence with the ark. In addition, the ark is viewed as both meeting place and place of ongoing divine instruction. The dynamics of encounter and communication are part of the theology of the tabernacle.

Finally, *Exod. 40:12-15* instructs Moses to bring Aaron and his sons to the tent in order to serve Yahweh as priests (cf. Exod. 29:44). The tabernacle is a place of ritual and, as such, requires a priesthood. It is viewed as the divine dwelling place, the place at which the divine-human encounter occurs, the place of divine instruction, and the place of ritual.

As already noted, the tabernacle must be located within the context of creation theology (Gorman 1993, 50-59). The parallels between the instructions for the construction of the tabernacle (Exod. 25–31) and the process of creation (Gen. 1:1–2:4a; see Kearney 1977; Levenson 1988, 80-86; Fretheim 1991, 268-72; Fishbane 1979, 11-13), the erection of the tabernacle on the first day of the first month (Exod. 40:17), and the concluding statement that "Moses finished the work" (Exod. 40:33b; cf. Gen. 2:2; see Blenkinsopp 1976, 280-83; Lohfink 1982), all suggest that the tabernacle is to be situated within the context of creation theology. It reflects God's ongoing creative activity in the world.

Holiness

One primary concern of priestly theology is holiness. Leviticus recognizes three interrelated aspects of holiness: the holiness associated with Yahweh; the holiness associated with the tabernacle (i.e., sacred or holy space); and the holiness enacted by the community (especially in Lev. 17–26). In the priestly traditions, holiness is a concrete manifestation of Yahweh in interaction with the world. Specifically, the holiness of Yahweh is associated with the glory of Yahweh (Exod. 29:43). The glory, in turn, is associated with the presence and manifestation of Yahweh in the fire and the cloud on Mt. Sinai (Exod. 24:15-18) and in the tabernacle (Exod. 40:34-38). In this way, Yahweh's holiness is made manifest in the tabernacle in the midst of Israel.

Yahweh dwells at the center of the holy place, which is also the center of the Israelite community — the holy of holies. The holiness of this place must be watched over, protected, and guarded in, by, and through ritual. Holiness radiates out, by degrees, from the holy of holies. Thus, the outer room of the tent proper is less holy than the holy of holies but more holy than the area outside the tent. The area around the outer altar, in the courtyard, is more holy than the area outside of the large tabernacle structure but less holy than the holy area within the inner tent. The camp outside the large tabernacle structure is less holy than the areas within but more holy than areas outside the camp. Thus, there are grades of holiness that radiate out from the holy of holies (see Milgrom 1991, 254-61; Jenson 1992, 89-114).

At the same time, holiness is a shared construct of the community and Yahweh. This can be seen in three texts. First, God made the sabbath day holy (Gen. 2:3), but God also calls on the Israelites to "make the Sabbath holy" (Lev. 23:3). The holiness of the sabbath is ritually constructed as well as divinely established. Second, Yahweh declares that the divine presence makes the tent of meeting holy (Exod. 29:43), but it also requires the ritual activity of Moses (Lev. 8:10-11). Third, Lev. 22:32 states that it is Yahweh who makes the people holy (cf. Exod. 19:6), but, at the same time, Yahweh demands that the community enact holiness in order to actualize it (Lev. 19:2; 20:7). The holiness of the community is both a declared state and an enacted state.

Finally, the community must enact holiness. Yahweh calls for Israel to be holy, in the same way that Yahweh is holy and gives instructions for how this is to be accomplished. The instructions focus primarily, although certainly not exclusively, on social relations. Holiness in community relations means interacting faithfully with other members of the community. This is one means of manifesting the divine life in the world. The call to holiness is a call to imitate Yahweh.

THE FRAMEWORK: LIFE AND DEATH/ORDER AND CHAOS

The world of priestly ritual, priestly community, and priestly theology is complex. No single image or idea is able to encompass and hold together the dynamic and tightly interwoven threads that make up the priestly traditions (see Nelson 1993, 17-38).

The priestly traditions seek to reflect on God, the community, and the world in the context of enactment, performance, holiness, and justice.

There are, however, two interrelated and dynamic sets of conceptual categories that provide a theological framework for much of this material. The first set of categories consists of the realm of life and the realm of death. Life was created and affirmed in the priestly account of creation (Gen. 1:1–2:4a). God blesses human beings and instructs them to create new life. Creativity, reproductive energy, and fertility are elements of lived experience. They provide the context in which humans live out and enact their lives. More specifically, the Israelite camp is viewed as the place of life. In this context, life is characterized by wholeness, well-being, prosperity, peace, community, and holiness.

Over against the realm of life stands the realm of death. Death is thought of in two ways. There is the actual death of the person — the cessation of life, the death of the body. Death means separation from home and community. It is the end of lived experience; it is the end of interaction with the world of the living. It is also separation from God. Death means the end of one's experience of God in the land of the living.

The realm of death, however, also intruded upon the community through the presence of a corpse (Num. 19:11), in the form of skin eruptions that caused the skin to look like that of a dead person (Lev. 13 and cf. Num. 12:10-15), through the abnormal discharge of fluids from the sexual organs (Lev. 15), in and through the birth process (Lev. 12), and even through sexual intercourse (Lev. 15:18). In each of these situations, "death" made its presence manifest in the life of the community. Contact with "the encroaching realm of death" creates impurity that pollutes and violates the holy area. Such contact can result in expulsion from the community for those with an unclean skin disease, with a bodily discharge, or who have come into contact with a corpse (Num. 5:2; cf. Lev. 13:45-46).

The second set of categories consists of order and chaos. In Gen. 1:1–2:4a, God constructs the very good order of creation out of chaos. Located within the order of creation, however, are aspects of the primordial chaos: darkness and the waters of the deep (Gen.

1:1-2; see Hyers 1984, 58-71). The original darkness rhythmically and endlessly covers the earth with the arrival of each night, and the waters endlessly stretch out their waves in an effort to reclaim the dry earth from which they were separated (Gen. 1:9-10). Chaos is an ever-present possibility for the Israelites, and they must watch over the order of creation in order to maintain and preserve it. Ritual is one means by which Israel accomplishes this.

Thus, the priestly traditions are concerned with creating life and maintaining order. Both are experienced within the context of the community. Both ritual enactments and social enactments are crucial to the construction and maintenance of order and the experience of life. Priestly rituals function to affirm life and to maintain the very good order of creation.

EXPIATION

Various forms of the Hebrew *k-p-r* appear in the priestly traditions. No single English word does justice to the range of meanings associated with the priestly use of *kpr* (Milgrom 1976b; 1991, 1079-84; Hartley 1992, 63-66). "Expiation" is used in the present work for the sake of convenience and consistency.

Etymologically, the word has been related to roots meaning "to cover," "to wipe off" or "to rub," and "to ransom." In priestly ritual, *kpr* has been thought to expiate sin (i.e., remove sin and its effects), to propitiate God (i.e., hold back the anger of God by providing a "ransom" for the sinner), or to effect atonement (i.e., to make "at one" with God; see Nelson 1993, 75). Usage must be considered, however, in addition to etymology. At the most general level, *kpr* means "to deal with disruptions in the divine-human relations." It does this in a variety of ways.

"Disruption" is used because there are several places in the priestly traditions in which sin is not involved, but the ritual process results in *kpr*. For example, the priest enacts expiation for a new mother, with the result that she becomes clean (Lev. 12:8b). The new mother has not sinned. Impurity associated with the blood of birth is the concern. The text clarifies the meaning of *kipper* by stating, "and she shall be clean" (cf. Lev. 15:15, 30).

Jacob Milgrom has argued persuasively that *kpr* is used in the context of the "purification offering" (*hatta't*, normally translated "sin offering"), to mean "purge" (1991, 226-318, 1079-84). What is purged, however, is not the sin of the individual but the impurity that has attached itself to the tabernacle. Central to his argument is the fact that the blood of the purification sacrifice is never placed on a person. Rather, it is placed on objects that are to be cleansed, for example, the tabernacle, the altar. The blood absorbs the impurity from the object and purges it (see Lev. 16:16a). Impurity and the possible departure of Yahweh from the midst of the community were the primary concerns of the priestly traditionists (see the comments on Lev. 4).

"Expiation" has been used to translate a variety of forms of the Hebrew *kpr*, but it must be understood in a very broad sense. It refers to the results of ritual *processes* that are enacted in order to deal with a variety of problems that arise in the context of the divine-human relationship. Rituals of expiation set right the relationship between God and the Israelites. Its specific meaning or nuance must be contextually determined.

LEVITICUS AND CHRISTIAN THEOLOGY

Christian theology has generally taken one of two approaches to the book of Leviticus. First, the rituals and laws of the book are viewed as expressions of an ancient religion. In this view, they are dismissed either as a remnant of a less developed past or as a legalistic construction of religion that is oppressive and contrary to grace. Second, they are viewed as a stage in the redemptive activity of God that culminated in the person and work of Jesus of Nazareth. In this view, either the rituals and laws are understood as indicators of the human need for a redeemer, or they are incorporated in the construction of a Christology that emphasizes the sacrificial nature of Jesus' death.

Both of these approaches, in their various configurations, are problematic for several reasons. First, they fail to take seriously the larger pentateuchal context of Leviticus and, thereby, fail to understand that Leviticus is part of Israel's story of God's grace enacted in the midst of and on behalf of the community. The divine instructions are viewed not as oppressive burdens but as actualizations of God's love and grace. Second, both views fail to understand the importance of the human enactment of holiness as a theological category. In particular, Christian readings of Leviticus often fail to recognize the ways in which God and the Israelite community share in the enactment and construction of holiness. Enactment, in Leviticus, includes both ritual enactment and ethical enactment. All of life is lived in the presence of Yahweh, who dwells in the midst of the community. To separate ethics from ritual is already to move to a fragmented view of life that is not found in Leviticus.

Third, both views assume the primacy and superiority of Christian theological categories and constructions. This perspective becomes problematic when these categories are imposed on Leviticus. This is not to say that Christianity should not have its own theological categories. Nor is it to suggest that these categories should be held in suspension while one reads Leviticus. It is to suggest, however, that Leviticus should be allowed the opportunity to provide its own categories for theological engagement. Thus, if one begins with the assumption that ritual is equivalent to law, and that law is an inferior form of religion, then Leviticus is disqualified as a constructive theological voice before the "reading" is even begun. One important theological category for any Christian reading of this material is "respect for its voice."

Finally, Christian theology has tended to read Leviticus from the viewpoint that Christianity has superseded and is superior to "Judaism." This approach generally views Leviticus as an early expression of Judaism (as if Leviticus and Judaism are equivalent!). Thus, Leviticus is devalued or is taken seriously only when it contributes to Christian concerns. This view reflects a long-standing bias in Christian theology against Judaism. Both Leviticus and Judaism, and the latter is not to be reduced to the former, have their own voice. A Christian reading of Leviticus must seek to hear the "voice" of Leviticus on its own terms. This is not to suggest that Christian readings of the book should be undertaken in a theological vacuum. Indeed, such readings are not possible in that all readings are to some extent located in the theological and ideological contexts of the reader. It is to argue that Leviticus must be engaged in its own terms.

A theological reading of Leviticus begins with the primary theme of the book: *the enactment of holiness in the context of a community that has the divine presence at its center.* Three aspects of the statement need discussion in terms of theology: enactment, community, and the presence of God.

Enactment

Leviticus recognizes that enactment is a significant aspect of human existence. In the Christian West, all too often human beings have been reduced to thinking and emoting beings. Human life, however, is constituted by activity and enactment. Ritual and ritualization are significant aspects of human existence as it is actually lived and experienced. Theology must retrieve enactment as a category of human existence. Related to this is the recognition in Leviticus that social enactments and ritual enactments are interconnected. There is no deep divide, no fragmentation, between one's enactments in the social world and one's enactments in the cultic world. Leviticus seeks to see all of life as a whole. Finally, Leviticus recognizes the importance of body for human existence. Western theology has rather consistently reflected a suspicion and devaluation of the body. Indeed, all too often Western theology has assumed a dichotomy between the mind and the body, which fails to do justice to human existence as actually lived and experienced. Leviticus seeks to take the body seriously. Contemporary readers will not agree with all of its rulings on the body, which many times are efforts to control and construct the body in very specific and narrow ways, but they should find in Leviticus a healthy recovery of physicality as an important theological category.

Community

Leviticus locates the individual in the context of the larger community. Human life is lived in the context of the larger community, and theological reflection and construction must take the community seriously. In this regard, Leviticus locates the individual within a community that lives in the context of a shared story. Enactments of the individual and the community are undertaken in the context of a story that includes promise, exodus, and covenant. It is the shared story that provides a specific theological nuance to the ritual and social enactments of the Israelite community. Finally, the community is called to manifest integrity, honesty, and trust in its interactions. A life lived before God is a life that respects and values other persons and engages those other persons with honesty and integrity.

The Presence of God

The primary theological image of Leviticus is the holy God dwelling in the midst of the Israelite community. Leviticus takes the concrete presence of God seriously and seeks to discover what it means to live life in the presence of the holy God. It believes that God is an active presence and participant in the life of the community. God is actively involved in the story of this community. God shares in the shared story of this community, and God participates in the actualization of the story. God enacts holiness in the context of the Israelite community; the community is called to share in this enactment of holiness. Finally, Leviticus views this God in the midst of Israel as creator and redeemer. The instructions of Leviticus are located within the narrative and theological contexts of creation, promise, exodus, and covenant. The God who dwells in the midst of the community is Creator, Friend, Redeemer, Storyteller, and Covenant Partner. The enactment of holiness takes place in the context of and in conjunction with this God and this community.

THE SACRIFICES AND OFFERINGS
Leviticus 1–7

Leviticus 1–7 consists of two separate series of instructions concerning sacrifices and offerings. The instructions are bracketed with an introductory statement (1:1-2) and a concluding, summary statement (7:37-38). The first series is found in Lev. 1:1–6:7 (Heb. 1:1–5:26), and the second is found in 6:8–7:36 (Heb. 6:1–7:36). The order in which the sacrifices are discussed differs in the two series. The instructions in Lev. 1–5 are directed at the whole community (1:2; 4:2). The second series is directed at the priesthood (6:9 [Heb. 6:2]; 6:25 [Heb. 6:18]). The summary statement in Lev. 7:37-38, however, locates all the instructions within the context of the whole community. These are instructions written for the whole community.

FIRST SERIES (1:1–6:7 [HEB. 1:1–5:26])

Introductory Verses (1:1-2)

Verses 1-2 introduce the instructions for the presentation of the sacrifices and offerings in Lev. 1–7 and indicate that "Yahweh called Moses and spoke to him from the tent of meeting" (1:1). The sacrificial instructions are an expression of the divine will, which Moses hears and delivers to the Israelite community (cf. Num. 7:89). In this tradition, the tent is viewed as the place of ongoing instruction (cf. Exod. 25:22; see "Tabernacle" in the Introduction).

An alternative tradition indicates that Yahweh delivered these instructions to Moses on Mt. Sinai (Lev. 7:37-38; cf. 25:1; 26:46; 27:34). Following the enactment of the covenant at Mt. Sinai,

Moses ascends the mountain, enters into the cloud of glory (Exod. 24:15-18), and receives the divine plan for the tabernacle (Exod. 25–31). Moses descends from the mountain, following the golden calf incident, with the tablets of the new covenant and with his face "shining" (Exod. 34:29-35). He will not again ascend the mountain to speak with Yahweh. The tabernacle is constructed (Exod. 35–40) and the glory of Yahweh, originally seen by the people on the mountain, takes up residence in the tent (Exod. 40:34-38). A number of significant parallels exist between Exod. 24:15–25:1 and Exod. 40:34–Lev. 1:1 (see Milgrom 1991, 136-39). Both texts emphasize that the glory seen on the mountain is now resident in the tabernacle.

Exodus 40:34-38 not only looks back to Exod. 24:15-18 but also points ahead to Num. 9:15-23. Three literary and theological issues are noted. First, Exod. 40:34-38 and Num. 9:15-23 bracket the "revelation" associated with Mt. Sinai (see Milgrom 1991, 139; Cohn 1981, 43-61). Second, Moses' entry into the cloud in Exod. 24:15-18 is a unique occurrence in Israel's sacred story. It comes in response to the divine-human covenant and in anticipation of the divine-human community. Third, and following from this, these texts emphasize the divine presence that is now in the midst of the community.

The instructional statement in v. 2 is general and introductory: "When any of you present an offering to Yahweh from the livestock, the offering that you present shall be from the herd or the flock." "Livestock" states the general category, which is further specified as animals from the herd or the flock, that is, bulls, goats, and sheep.

The Burnt Offering (1:3-17)

Introduction

In the burnt offering (*'olah*) the animal is wholly burned on the altar (the skin of the animal, however, goes to the officiating priest, Lev. 7:8). Emphasis is placed on the "going up" of the smoke. The precise function of the burnt offering is difficult to determine because of its long history.

The text states that the rising smoke of the burnt offering

provides "a soothing aroma for Yahweh" (vv. 9; 13; 17; cf. Num. 15:3, 13; 28:2). Yahweh has been unsettled or disturbed, and the rising smoke of the burnt offering provides a soothing fragrance. In addition, v. 4 states that the burnt offering "expiates." The priestly traditions generally limit the expiatory power of the burnt offering to larger ritual processes that include other sacrifices and offerings (e.g., Lev. 9:7; 14:20; 16:24). In these traditions the expiatory power of the burnt offering is primarily concerned with the "wrath" of Yahweh (cf. the following nonpriestly texts, Deut. 29:28; Jer. 21:5; 32:31; 2 Chron. 19:10; 24:18; 29:8; Isa. 54:8; Zech. 7:12). For example, in Num. 16:41-50 (Heb. 17:6-15), following the death of Korah and the other rebels, Yahweh is angered by the people and threatens to consume them (16:45 [Heb. 17:10]). Moses instructs Aaron to take fire from the altar, to put it in a censer with incense, and then to go and enact expiation *(wekapper)* for the people "because the wrath has gone out from before Yahweh — the plague has begun" (v. 46 [Heb. v. 11]). The sin of the people antagonizes Yahweh, who responds with wrath. "Expiation" *(kpr)* has to do with holding back the wrath of Yahweh and soothing him.

Numbers 18:5 states that Aaron and his sons are responsible for performing their prescribed duties in relation to the sanctuary and the altar so that wrath will not come upon the Israelites. The sudden "going forth" of the wrath of Yahweh is a very real possibility, and ritual processes must address it. The burnt offering functions to prevent the outbreak of Yahweh's wrath.

The "very good" order of creation provides the theological context for the wrath of God. Divine wrath reflects an offended creator as well as a righteous judge. A disruption of the right and good order of creation, be it cosmic, social, or cultic, offends and angers the divine creator. The burnt offering provides a pleasing fragrance for God and cools down the divine wrath. A few instances in the priestly traditions associate the burnt offering with joy and thanksgiving (see Lev. 22:17-19; Num. 15:1-16), a response to the peaceful relationship that exists with God.

In addition, the burnt offering functions as a daily maintenance ritual. Exodus 29:38-46 prescribes that a burnt offering is to be presented every morning and every evening. These daily sacrifices mark out, "re-member," and maintain the initial act of creation: the creation of light and the separation of the light from the darkness (Gen. 1:4-5). The morning and evening sacrifices function as ritual markers of this original act of creation. The preservation and maintenance of that order is central to the ongoing presence of God in the midst of Israel. The daily sacrifices are also reminders that God brought Israel out of Egypt. The God of the Exodus is also the God of creation and the God with whom the Israelite community interacts in the tabernacle ritual. This God has called the Israelite community into being in order to dwell in its midst (see vv. 42-46).

The Ritual Proper

Leviticus 1:3-17 specifies three types of animals that may be offered: a male without blemish from the herd (vv. 3-9), a male without blemish from the flock (vv. 10-13), or an offering of birds (vv. 14-17). The three options are related to the economic ability of the offerer. The structure of the ritual is similar for all three types: presentation of the animal, the slaughter and blood manipulation, the flaying and burning. Six verbs prescribe the ritual actions: *offer* the animal → *lay* a hand on the animal's head → *slaughter* the animal → *present* the blood → *flay* the animal → *burn* the animal. These six activities move the animal from the offerer to Yahweh and enact a ritual process that culminates in a soothing aroma for Yahweh.

The Presentation (vv. 3-4): Verses 3-4 provide the primary details for the presentation of the sacrifice. The offerer is to bring the animal to the altar at the entrance of the tent of meeting (v. 3). This altar is sometimes called "the altar of burnt offerings" (e.g., Exod. 38:1; 40:6; Lev. 4:7b [used here to distinguish it from the altar of incense, which is inside the tent and on which, according to Exod. 30:9, sacrifices are forbidden]). "The entrance of the tent" designates a ritually constructed and defined space, the place at which the people bring and offer their sacrifices to Yahweh. Indeed, in the priestly traditions, sacrificial activity is normally only undertaken at the entrance to the tent of meeting. The "entrance of the tent" is the place where the divine and human intersect, the sacred and the mundane come together. It is important to recognize that ritual space reflects the history and life of Israel. God and humans come together in the actualization of the story that they share. In ritual, God and the people come together to construct, enact, and actualize a community that is identified not only in, by, and through its story but also in, by, and through its ritual.

The offerer brings the animal to the entrance where the hand-laying rite takes place. In this case, the hand-laying rite does not function to transfer the sins of the offerer to the animal, as it does, for example, in Lev. 16:21-22 (see Milgrom 1976b, 765; Péter 1977, 54-55). In this case, the hand-laying rite functions as an act of presentation and identification. It is the moment in the larger ritual process when the offerer presents the animal to the priest and identifies the animal as an offering brought for Yahweh. The hand-laying rite functions to make the animal acceptable for its role in a ritual designed to effect expiation (v. 4). The whole ritual process — the presentation, the hand-laying, the slaughter, the blood manipulation, the flaying, and the burning — accomplishes expiation; the presentation begins the process.

Slaughter and Blood Manipulation (vv. 5, 11, 15): The offerer is to slaughter the animal (v. 5a) on the north side of the altar (v. 11a). The act of slaughter is central to the ritual process, and it is the responsibility of the offerer to perform the slaughter. The offerer brings the animal to the entrance of the tent, identifies it as a sacrificial animal, moves it into the realm of the sacred, and then slaughters it. At the heart of the ritual interaction of Yahweh and Israel is the slaughter of animals in the context of the sacred.

The priest throws the blood against the sides of the altar. The precise significance of the blood rite in this ritual is not clear. Two conceptual issues must be considered. The first is the prohibition against eating flesh with the blood in it because the life of the animal is in its blood (Gen. 9:4). In a different context, the blood prohibition is related to the expiatory function of the blood on the altar (Lev. 17:10-12; v. 11; see the discussion of this verse in ch. 17). The ritual processes of expiation "work" because the blood that is placed on the altar "contains" the life of the animal. The animal's "life" is passed from the everyday world of the offerer to the realm of the sacred and Yahweh. The second conceptual category is the priestly concern for maintaining the boundary between life and death (see the discussions of chs. 12 and 14). The priests would view the slaughter of an animal in the context of ritual as a "dangerous" activity. A "reckoning" is associated with the killing of an animal (see Gen. 9:4-6). The placement of the blood of slaughtered animals on the altar must be understood within these multiple contexts. The presentation of the blood is necessary because an animal has been killed for ritual purposes. The slaughter of an animal in the context of the sacred is made possible, one might say is made "safe," through the placement of its life, which is in its blood, on the altar.

The Burning (vv. 6-9, 12-13, 16-17): The offerer cuts the animal into pieces and washes its entrails and legs with water since these parts might be defiled through contact with waste materials. The priest prepares the altar with wood and fire and arranges the pieces of the animal on the altar. The whole animal is turned into smoke.

The Ritual for Birds (vv. 14-17): The ritual process for birds varies a bit because of their physical characteristics. The hand-laying rite is not necessary because the bird is brought "in the hand" and given to the priest. The priest wrings off its head and drains its blood against the side of the altar (v. 15). The crop and related parts are to be removed (Milgrom argues [1991, 169-71] that this refers to the lower digestive tract, which may be removed by the tail feather). The priest then tears the bird, without severing it in half, and turns it into smoke on the altar (v. 17).

The Grain Offering (2:1-16)

Introduction

The grain offering *(minha)* is often viewed as a cheaper form of the burnt offering. The uncertain historical development of these offerings makes precision impossible. Only parts of the cereal offering are burned on the altar, in contrast to the "whole" burnt offering. In addition, it is not clear that a grain offering could accomplish expiation (see the discussion of 1:4 above) in that the *blood* of an animal is not placed on the altar (see 17:11). The text states, however, that the purpose of the grain offering, like the burnt offering, is to provide "a soothing aroma for Yahweh" (v. 2).

There are only three instances in which a grain offering is to be offered independently of other sacrifices: a grain offering of firstfruits (2:14-16; cf. 23:9-14); a grain offering associated with the ordination of the priests (6:19-23 [Heb. 6:12-16], although this is probably associated with the daily presentations of the burnt offering [see Exod. 29:38-42; Num. 28:1-8]); and the grain offering of jealousy, also termed the grain offering of remembrance, associated with a husband's charge of unfaithfulness (Num. 5:11-28). The grain offering is normally located within a larger ritual process that includes additional sacrifices and offerings (e.g., Lev. 7:11-14; 8:25-29; 14:20; 23:16-19; Num. 6:16-17; 15:1-21; 28:8, 9, 11-12, 19-20). The grain offering is considered to be "most holy" (Lev. 6:17 [Heb. 6:10]), as are the burnt offering, purification offering, and reparation offering (see Lev. 6:17 [10], 25 [18]; 7:6).

The priestly traditions may envision two distinct situations for the grain offering. In one, the grain offering is presented by itself and functions as an expression of joy or thanksgiving. In the other, the grain offering is part of a larger ritual process. In these ritual processes, the offerer brings both animals and grain to the sanctuary to present to Yahweh. The Israelites would have felt the importance of these presentations. These signs of blessing became empowered when presented in the context of the sacred. The contemporary reader often fails to appreciate the lives of real persons who take animals from their own farms and grain from their own gardens in order to hand them over to Yahweh in the context of the sacred. The experiential rhythms of life are played out at the entrance of the tent. Real human stories draw near to Yahweh. The divine story and the human story become merged and shared.

The ritual of the grain offering is not as complex as that of the burnt offering. The instructions focus primarily on details related to the preparation of the offering. The chapter consists of two parallel statements on grain offerings (vv. 1-3 and vv. 4-10), prohibitions against the inclusion of leaven or honey in offerings to be placed on the altar (vv. 11-12), a prescription to include

27

salt in the offerings (v. 13), and a statement on the grain offering of firstfruits (vv. 14-16).

The Ritual Proper (vv. 1-3, 8-10)

The structure of the ritual for the grain offering is similar in each instance: preparation, presentation, and the burning of the representative portion.

Preparation: The preparation of the grain offering is part of the larger ritual process. This is indicated by the detailed discussion given to the preparation of the various types of grain offerings. Five distinct types are noted: (1) uncooked fine flour (vv. 1-3) or grain (vv. 14-16); (2) thin cakes of unleavened flour baked in an oven (v. 4); (3) unleavened wafers baked in the oven (v. 4); (4) cakes of unleavened bread prepared on a griddle (v. 5); and (5) flour cooked in a pan (v. 7). Many details are left unspecified. The fact that the preparation is completed away from the tent does not disqualify it as ritualized activity. It is incorrect to argue that the ritual only begins at the time of presentation. Such a view removes ritual from the dynamics of life. The instructions for the grain offerings provide a framework for the enactment of the ritual that intersects with the rhythms of daily life.

The two uncooked offerings — the uncooked offering of choice flour (vv. 1-3) and the grain offering of firstfruits (vv. 14-16) — require oil and frankincense. Frankincense is not included in the cooked offerings of vv. 4-10 (cf. Num. 15:1-10, which indicates that frankincense was not required for grain offerings presented in conjunction with blood sacrifices). Oil, however, is to be included.

Presentation: The text says very little about the presentation of the grain offering to the priest. The one who makes the offering either "brings" (v. 2) or "presents" (v. 8) it to the priest (v. 8). "Bringing" and "presenting" mark the movement of the offering from the hand of the offerer to the hand of the priest, from the mundane to the sacred.

Burning the Representative Portion: The priest takes a representative portion of the offering and turns it into smoke on the altar. The remainder of the grain offering belongs to the priest. The "representative portion" *(ʾazkarah)* takes the place of and represents the whole offering. In the uncooked offerings, the priest burns a handful of the flour/grain, oil, and all of the frankincense (vv. 2, 16). This provides the soothing fragrance for Yahweh. With the cooked offerings, the priest simply removes the representative portion, about a handful if the uncooked offerings provide an accurate model, and burns it on the altar.

Special Instructions (vv. 11-13)

Verses 11-12 state that neither leaven nor honey are to be included in any offering turned into smoke on the altar. In the priestly view, the fermentation associated with leaven brought it into connection with decay and corruption and, thus, with death. The prohibition of leaven reflects the priestly concern to maintain firm boundaries between life and death so as to insure the ongoing separation of these two realms. The same reasoning applies to the prohibition of honey. It is probable that fruit honey is intended because of the fermentation associated with it (Milgrom 1991, 189-90). The altar must be protected from items associated with decay, corruption, and death.

Salt is to be offered with all the offerings. It is referred to as the "salt of the covenant" (v. 13; cf. the phrase in Num. 18:19 and 2 Chron. 13:5). This phrase most likely refers to covenants that have binding and perpetual qualities. If so, the salt in the sacrifices serves as a constant reminder of the covenant relationship that exists between Yahweh and Israel.

The Firstfruits of Grain (vv. 14-16)

The grain offering of firstfruits discussed in vv. 14-16 is best understood as an offering of barley (Milgrom 1991, 192-93; cf. Lev. 23:9-14 and Deut. 26:9-10). It follows the basic pattern for grain offerings. In that the offering of firstfruits was not optional, the text should read "when" you bring your offering of firstfruits (v. 14). This offering provides an excellent example of the way in which ritual enactment takes place within the context of the daily rhythms of life. The offerer works the land that belongs to Yahweh (see Lev. 25:23-24), brings the firstfruits of the land to the sacred place, and presents it to the priest, who turns the representative portion into smoke on the altar. It is an enactment of the relationship that exists between Yahweh, the people, and the land.

The Well-being Offering (3:1-17)

Introduction

The well-being offering *(zebah shelamim)* has a long and varied history that is difficult to reconstruct. Each of the two words may be used individually to refer to sacrifices (for *shelamim,* see Lev. 6:12 [5]; 7:14, 33; Num. 6:14; 15:8; for *zebah,* see Lev. 17:5, 7, 8; 19:6; 23:37; Num. 15:3, 5, 8), although the priestly traditionists normally use them together. The two words have distinctive meanings. *Zebah* is related to the word for "altar" *(mizbeah)* and refers to a slain sacrifice. The meat of an animal offered as a *zebah* is eaten by the offerer and relatives. In some instances, *zebah* is combined with other words to specify a particular type of sacrifice: for example, "sacrifices of thanksgiving" (Ps. 107:22; 116:17), "the yearly sacrifice" (1 Sam. 1:21), "a family sacrifice" (1 Sam. 20:29), and "the Passover sacrifice" (Ex. 12:27; 34:25). A variety of suggestions have been offered to explain the meaning of *shelamim:* for example, peace offering, concluding offering, communion sacrifice, and covenant sacrifice (see the brief reviews in Wenham 1979, 76-81 and Milgrom 1991, 220-22). The present discussion will use "well-being offering."

The priestly traditions only *require* the presentation of the well-being sacrifice in two instances: at the inaugural ritual of the newly ordained priesthood (Lev. 9:18-21) and at the feast of weeks (23:19). The priestly traditions specify three distinct types of well-being offerings: the thanksgiving offering *(nebada),* the votive offering *(neder),* and the freewill offering *(todah; 7:11-18).* Each of these indicates a situation in which the offerer is making a response of gratitude and joy to God. The well-being sacrifice is a way of enacting that response.

The sacrificial system must be related to and understood within the context of the dynamics of Israelite life. The well-being sacrifice is a ritual means of enacting one's gratitude and joy and of positioning the self within the context of the sacred. Just as the psalms reflect the voice of real persons living in and through real situations and bringing their experiences to God through song and prayer (see Brueggemann 1995), so ritual involves real persons who emerge out of real life experiences and come to the sanctuary in order to situate their lives within the context of the sacred. Ritual is a means for enacting human experience in the context of the sacred.

Although the overall structure of the ritual of the well-being offering is similar to that of the burnt offering, there are significant differences (see 7:11-18, 28-36 for additional information on the well-being sacrifice). First, only specific portions of the animal's fat are burned in the well-being offering. Second, the worshipper eats parts of the well-being offering. The well-being offering is not said to be expiatory, although the smoke of the burned fat provides a soothing aroma for Yahweh (vv. 5, 16) and it is called a food offering by fire for Yahweh (*lehem 'ishsheh;* vv. 11, 16). The offerer and Yahweh share in the "consumption" of this sacrifice.

The chapter specifies the animals that may be used for a well-being sacrifice: an animal from the herd, male or female, (vv. 1-5); an animal from the flock, either a sheep, male or female (vv. 6-11); or a goat (vv. 12-16). Each unit begins with the phrase, "if your offering is" (vv. 1, 6, 12), and concludes with an indication that the sacrifice has been accepted by Yahweh (vv. 5, 11, 16). A concluding statement prohibits the Israelite consumption of any fat or blood (vv. 16b-17).

The Ritual Proper

The larger ritual process has four basic movements: (1) presentation and the hand-laying rite; (2) slaughter and blood manipulation; (3) the burning of the fat; and (4) the sacrificial meal.

The Presentation (vv. 1-2, 6-8a, 12-13a): The bringing of the animal to the tabernacle, the hand-laying rite, and the presentation to the priest have been discussed in relation to the burnt offering. These actions very likely carry the same function in this ritual. It must be recognized, however, that a specific ritual may nuance a particular act in a distinctive way (see "Theology and Ritual in Leviticus" in the Introduction).

The Slaughter and Blood Manipulation (vv. 2, 8, 13): See the discussion of these in relation to the burnt offering.

The Burning (vv. 3-5, 9-11, 14-16): The text indicates precisely the portions of fat and the organs that are to be burned on the altar: the fat that is around and connected to the entrails, the two kidneys with the fat around them along with the sinews (see Milgrom 1991, 207), and the small protuberance that extends down from the liver. If the offering is a sheep, the removed portions must include "the broad tail" (v. 9), a reference to the broad-tailed sheep found in Palestine (Milgrom 1991, 210-12). The text states that the fat belongs to Yahweh and is forbidden for human consumption (vv. 16b-17). It does not, however, explain *why* this is the case.

The fat is burned on the altar to provide a soothing aroma for Yahweh. The statement that the fat is to be burned on the altar "with the burnt offering already on the wood" indicates that this sacrifice is placed on top of the regular morning burnt offering (see Exod. 29:38-42). The sacrifice is termed a "food offering" (vv. 11, 16), and the burning is followed by a sacrificial meal. The central feature of this ritual is the sharing of the animal — God smells the burning of the fat and the offerer eats the meat.

The Sacrificial Meal (see Lev. 7:11-18, 28-36): The sense of sharing a meal is at the heart of the imagery of this ritual. This is not a spiritualizing of the sacrifice; it is a ritualizing of the meal. The experience of communion is crucial. To be sure, there is no indication of a merging of the divine and the human in mystic union. The "coming together" is not, however, merely symbolic. It is the enactment of communion shared through the meal. In this way the ritual strikes deep emotions — joy and celebration are enacted in the context of the sacred and of a shared meal. The ritual process recognizes the emotional life of people and provides the opportunity for the expression of the emotional life in the context of the holy. The everyday life of the person is connected with the sacred in such a way that both the everyday life of the offerer and the divine life of Yahweh are transformed.

Concluding Prohibition (vv. 16b-17)

The concluding prohibition states: "All fat belongs to Yahweh . . . you must not eat any fat or any blood" (vv. 16b-17). The blood prohibition is first found in the priestly story of the flood and its

aftermath (Gen. 9:4-5) and is further explicated in Lev. 17:10-13
— God has given it to Israel to place on the altar in order to effect
expiation (see the discussion of Lev. 17). The fat and the blood
belong to Yahweh. Since blood is associated with life, it is likely,
although not certain, that fat has a similar connotation. Those
parts of the animal associated with life belong to God. This
prohibition is termed "a perpetual statute" (v. 17; cf. 7:36; 10:9;
16:29, 34; 17:7; 23:14, 21, 31, 41; 24:3). This indicates the
extremely important nature of these particular instructions.

The Purification Offering (4:1–5:13)

The purification offering *(hatta't)* has often been termed "the
sin offering." This designation is too general and incorrectly
places the emphasis on sin. "Purification" more precisely indicates
its primary function within the priestly sacrificial system (Wenham
1979, 86-101; Milgrom 1991, 253-92). This sacrifice functions
to purify the tabernacle from impurity generated by the life of
the community, to restore the sacred status of the holy area, and
to bring about forgiveness for the person or persons responsible
for the sin that generated defiling impurity (if sin was involved).

Leviticus 4:1–5:13 details three distinct types of purification
offerings. The first type is discussed in 4:3-21 and applies to "the
anointed priest" (vv. 3-12) or "the whole congregation" (vv.
13-21). The second type is discussed in 4:22-35 and applies to "a
ruler" (vv. 22-26) or "anyone of the ordinary people" (vv. 27-35).
The third type is discussed in 5:1-13 and involves four situations
that require a purification offering. A scale of sacrificial materials
based on a person's economic means is constructed. It is best not
to seek an ideal ritual pattern or a single structural and functional
definition for these ritual processes. The rituals address problems
associated with impurity caused by the ongoing life of the community. These instructions provide a framework for enacting and
effecting purification, restoration, and forgiveness.

Introduction

Leviticus 4:1-2 provides a general introductory statement, which
indicates the primary situation that requires a purification offer-

ing: a person (or the community) does something inadvertently that is prohibited by the commandments of Yahweh, for example, a sin of commission. Leviticus 5:1-4 focuses on sins of omission: a person has failed to do something that should have been done. Thus, the purification offering addresses both sins of commission and sins of omission.

In addition, a purification offering is required in several cases in which no sin has been committed, for example, the priestly ordination ritual (ch. 8), the purification process for a new mother (ch. 12), and the ritual for the recovered leper (ch. 13). The purification offering not only is concerned with sin but also functions within the context of the priestly impurity system. Modern categories of "moral," "ethical," and "ceremonial" must be used with caution, if at all.

In Lev. 4, sins that require a purification offering must be "inadvertent" or "unintentional" (Heb. *bishgagah;* vv. 2, 13, 22, 27). In addition, the offending party must experience and recognize "guilt" (vv. 3, 13-14, 22-23, 27-28). Although the word "inadvertent" is lacking in the cases specified in 5:1-4, the suspicion, experience, or recognition of guilt is crucial (see Milgrom 1967; Kiuchi 1987, 25-31; Levine 1989, 19-23).

In terms of inadvertancy, a person might either commit an act without knowing that it is wrong or, knowing an act to be wrong, fail to recognize that it has been committed. The key is that a person (or the community) does something that is not to be done, but does it without knowledge or malicious intent. The act is not committed in an effort to disobey Yahweh. This is in contrast to high-handed, intentional, and malicious sin (see Num. 15:27-31). The person who commits a high-handed sin is to be "cut off" *(hikkaret tikkaret)* and bear the guilt of the act (Num. 15:31; see Lev. 7:19-21 for a detailed discussion of "cut off"). Such a person despises the word of Yahweh and regards it contemptuously; that person maliciously, willfully, and intentionally disregards the commandments of Yahweh.

Finally, the priestly understanding of "guilt" *('ashem)* must be discussed (see Milgrom 1976a; Kiuchi 1987, 31-38; Hartley 1992, 76-80). In Hebrew, the word for "guilt" can refer both to an act by which one incurs guilt and to the feeling of guilt that is the consequence of such an act. In cases requiring a purification offering, a person has committed a sin without malicious intention or knowledge that the act was sinful, and then at a later time either comes to feel guilt or to recognize the guilt associated with the action. The person either has the wrong explained or begins to feel the guilt associated with the act. The purification offering is a ritual response to the moment of recognition and remorse (the situations detailed in Lev. 5:1-4 will be discussed below).

One primary function of the purification offering is to purify the sanctuary (sacred space) (8:14-15; 15:31; 16:15-19). Sin and certain situations create impurity, an invisible but powerful entity, that is attracted to and attaches itself to the tabernacle. The purification offering cleanses sacred space of this impurity (see Milgrom 1991, 253-92). Two aspects of this view must be noted. First, if the impurity is not ritually cleansed, its presence may force the departure of Yahweh from the midst of the people. This poses a threat to the identity and existence of the Israelite community. Yahweh cannot dwell in the midst of impurity and pollution (cf. Ezekiel's vision of the departure of the glory of Yahweh from the temple in Ezek. 8–10). Second, responsibility for addressing impurity is placed entirely on the people. The ongoing presence of Yahweh in the midst of the community is significantly related to the life of the people. Ritual provides one context for the interaction of Yahweh and Israel in their mutual quest for a holy community.

The purification offering for inadvertent sins can be placed in the following theological context. A person has committed an offense against Yahweh. Two problems arise: the offender incurs guilt and impurity is generated that pollutes the tabernacle, the dwelling place of Yahweh. The ritual *process* must deal both with the incurred guilt and the impurity of the sanctuary.

The Ritual Proper
The ritual process of the purification offering reflects the following structure: presentation, slaughter and blood manipulation, burning of the fat, and the disposal/eating of the remains. The manipulation of the blood is the crucial element in this ritual.

There are, however, variations in the manipulation of the blood that depend on the status of the offerer, the nature of the sacrificial context, and the type of animal sacrificed.

Presentation and Slaughter (vv. 4, 14-15, 23-24, 28-29, 32-33): The presentation of the animal, the hand-laying rite, and the slaughter function in the same way as in the burnt offering and the well-being offering (see the discussion of ch. 1). Note should be made of the offerer and the type of animal to be offered: "the anointed priest" and "the whole congregation" must bring a bull (vv. 3, 14); "a ruler" must bring a male goat (v. 23); "one of the ordinary people" must bring either a female goat (v. 28) or a female sheep (v. 32).

The Blood Manipulation (vv. 5-7, 16-18, 25, 30, 34): Discussion of the manipulation of the blood must examine three separate ritual contexts: (1) the regular sacrifice for a ruler or ordinary person (4:25, 30), (2) the more complex sacrifice for a priest or the whole community (4:5-7, 16-18), and (3) the sacrifice on the annual day of purification (16:11-19). In most cases, the purification sacrifice is part of a larger ritual process.

The sacrifice for a ruler (4:22-26) or an ordinary person (4:27-31) is the most basic form of the sacrifice. In this case, two distinct acts are involved: (1) some of the blood is placed on the horns of the altar and (2) the rest is poured out at the base of the altar. The blood placed on the horns of the altar functions to *purify* the altar of impurity that has arisen because of sin, while the blood poured out at the base of the altar functions to *reconsecrate* the altar. The pouring of the blood at the base of the altar is more than an act of disposal. The priests would not include this action in the context of ritual prescriptions if it did not have ritual significance.

Leviticus 8 can help clarify the issue. It describes the ordination of the priesthood and the consecration of sacred space. The purification offering follows the pattern for an ordinary person — Aaron and his sons are in the process of becoming priests, but they are not yet priests. This is the first actual presentation of the purification offering, and Moses, who functions here as founder and inaugurator of the tabernacle cult, enacts the priestly role (see Gorman 1990, 141-49). In what may be viewed as a founding ritual, the text is very explicit in explaining the actions. The blood of the bull is placed on the horns of the altar in order to purify the altar. The rest of the blood is poured out at the base of the altar in order to sanctify ("make holy") or reconsecrate it (Gorman 1990, 81-89).

The ritual construction of sacred space as prescribed in chs. 8–9 emphasizes that the tabernacle area was both holy *and* clean (on the relationship of these two categories, see Wenham 1979, 18-25; Levine 1989, 256-57; Hartley 1992, 141-46). A violation of the area by the impurity arising from sin disrupts not only its purity but also its holiness. Both the purity and the holiness of the tabernacle were ritually constructed and are subject to further ritual manipulation. The manipulation of the blood of the purification offering both purifies *and* makes holy.

In the ritual for a priest (4:3-12) or the whole congregation (4:13-21), the blood is brought inside the tent (see vv. 5-7). The impurity generated by the anointed priest or the whole community moves past the outer altar and enters into the tent itself (Milgrom 1991, 254-58). Three elements associated with the manipulation of the blood are of note: (1) it is sprinkled seven times before the curtain that marks off the holy of holies; (2) it is placed on the horns of the altar of incense inside the tent; (3) it is poured out at the base of the altar of burnt offering at the entrance of the tent.

The blood placed on the horns of the altar and poured out at the base of the outer altar functions to effect purification and reconsecration. The precise function of the sevenfold sprinkling rite is not certain (sprinkling rites are also found in Lev. 5:9; 8:11; 14:7, 16, 27, 51; 16:14, 19; Num. 19:4; see Gorman 1990, 83-86). In the present ritual, it has been interpreted as an act of consecration (Vriezen 1950), although why this would be necessary is not apparent. It has also been argued that the blood is actually being directed at the ark behind the curtain so that the curtain, being crafted with patterns similar to those on the ark, is understood to represent the ark (Kiuchi 1987, 119-30). It is not common, however, for the priestly traditions to have one object stand for another in matters of purification (i.e., the blood purifies by contact). In addition, the text does not make a connection between the curtain and the ark.

It is more likely that the curtain represents the boundary of the holy space that has been polluted (i.e., the outer room of the tent). The ritual cleanses and reconsecrates from the curtain, which is inside the tent, to the altar, which is outside the tent. The blood placed on the horns of the incense altar purifies and reconsecrates it, but the actual space of the inner room is bounded by the curtain. Thus, the sprinkling "on" the curtain functions to purify it (see Gorman 1990, 81-89).

The third purification offering with a distinct blood rite is enacted on the annual day of purification (see the detailed discussion of Lev. 16). In this ritual, blood is taken into the most holy space and sprinkled *on* and *before* the seat of expiation located on top of the ark. The blood is then brought outside the tent, placed on the horns of the altar, and sprinkled seven times on it. The two extremes of sacred space — the ark and the outer altar — receive ritual action. The very heart of the most holy place is sprinkled, top and bottom as it were, and the outer extreme, the altar of burnt offerings, is smeared and sprinkled. The ark in the holy of holies is the center of the holy space, and its holiness radiates out. Holy space "from stem to stern" is touched with the blood in order to purify and reconsecrate it (see v. 19).

The ritual process of purification and reconsecration of sacred space must be related to creation theology. The construction of the tabernacle (Exod. 40; Lev. 8–9) is part of the larger process of creation that is shared by Yahweh and Israel (see the Introduction). Sin creates impurity that violates and disrupts this clean and holy space. The order of creation is thereby violated. Ritual enactment is a means of re-creating the world, the divine-human relationship, and the holiness of the divine dwelling place.

The Burning of the Fat (vv. 8-10, 19, 26, 31, 35): The burning of the fat follows the same procedures as found in the well-being sacrifices (see the discussion in ch. 3). It provides a "soothing aroma" for Yahweh (v. 31).

The Disposal/Eating of the Remains (vv. 11-12, 21; 6:24-30 [Heb. 6:17-23]): There are two basic methods for disposing of the remains of the "purification" animal. First, if the blood is taken inside the tent, the remains are taken outside the camp "to a clean place" and burned (4:11-12; 21). The general rule for this is stated in 6:30, and it applies to the purification offerings for the anointed priest, the whole community, and those offered on the annual day of purification (16:27). In addition, the remains of the animals used in the priestly ordination ritual and in the inaugural activity of the priests are taken outside the camp and burned (Exod. 29:14; Lev. 8:17; 9:11). In the last two instances, the blood is *not* taken inside the tent. Second, if the blood is *not* taken inside the tent, the priests must eat at least some of the remains of the animal (Lev. 6:26; see the dispute over this issue in 10:16-20).

The elimination of the remains of the animal constitute an important element of the ritual process. The blood of the animal purifies by absorbing impurity, which is then communicated to the remains of the animal. The animal has been placed in the context of the holy through its presentation to Yahweh, but the remains are unclean because of its purificatory activity (see Milgrom 1991, 254-58; Kiuchi [1987, 130-42] emphasizes the death of the animal within the context of the holy and the priestly task of bearing the sin of the Israelites). Both the burning of the animal and the eating of some of it function to eliminate the impurity associated with the remains (see 10:17). Ritual provides the context for unifying the holy and the impure so that a new state — one that is both clean and holy — may come into being. Thus, purification, reconsecration, and elimination are all aspects of this ritual process. Rituals that require the blood to be brought into the tent address concerns relating to the impurity of the priests. The remains of these animals must be burned because the priests cannot consume their own impurities (Kiuchi 1987, 130-42; Milgrom 1991, 261-64). This explains, as well, why the purification sacrifices in the priestly ordination ritual and the inaugural sacrifices were burned outside the camp (Exod. 29:14; Lev. 8:17; 9:11).

Ritual Process, Expiation, and Forgiveness (vv. 20, 26, 31, 35)
The concluding phrase indicates that more than just purification of sacred space is involved in this ritual: "and you will be forgiven" (4:20, 26, 31, 35). The whole ritual process functions to effect forgiveness for the person. A person has sinned inadvertently, has

come to recognize and feel the guilt associated with the wrong-doing, and has enacted a ritual process designed to purify sacred space and to effect forgiveness. Forgiveness here means to re-structure and to set right a relationship. It is based on recognition of guilt and enactment of confession in a ritual context. This is not done, however, to forget or pass over what has taken place. It is done to restructure the situation and to enable the offender to move on in life (Milgrom 1981).

The Graduated Purification Offering (5:1-13)

The third type of purification sacrifice is a graduated purification sacrifice (Milgrom 1991, 292-318). The offerer is able to present a sacrifice relative to her or his economic ability: a female from the flock, either a sheep or a goat (5:6); two turtledoves or two pigeons, one for a sin offering and one for a burnt offering (5:7); or one-tenth of an ephah of choice flour (5:11). This text begins by specifying the offenses that call for a graded purification offer-ing. These cases are concerned with "sins of omission."

Four basic situations are detailed. The first case (5:1) states that a person who has heard a public call for testimony and who is able to testify knowledgeably but does not speak must bear the guilt *(nasa' 'awon)* of this failure to act. The second case (5:2) concerns contact with an impure thing, especially the carcass of an animal. The third case (5:3) concerns contact with human uncleanness, and the fourth case (5:4) addresses the problem of making a rash oath.

A basic pattern is present. A person has become guilty but is unaware of it. This is not an inadvertent sin (dealt with in ch. 4). In these cases, the person knew what was done but has forgotten about it and is unaware of the problem. Nonetheless, the person is guilty. Verse 5 is crucial: "And when the person comes to recognize or feel the guilt associated with any of these situations, then that person must confess the sin that has been committed." Recognition of guilt brings with it the responsibility to make a public confession and then to undertake the appropriate offering (detailed in vv. 6-13).

In the first case, the person has failed to testify within a specified time. The problem in this case is that a person "intentionally" refuses to testify in the context of an oath. In Israel, because an oath is made in the context of the sacred, the person who disregards the oath and refuses to respond dishonors God. It is probable that the issue in the second and third cases has to do with failure to undertake appropriate purification practices (see the details in Lev. 11:24-40; Num. 19; 31:19). Such negligence and delay result in greater impurity (Milgrom 1991, 307-18). In the fourth case, the problem arises when the person fails to fulfill an oath within its stated time. The instructions make allowances for these situations and state that a person, upon experiencing the guilt associated with one of these "failures," may confess and present an offering to obtain purification and forgiveness.

These four cases involve a distinct purification offering that requires confession (Milgrom 1991, 300-303, 373-78). The offering is based on a person's economic abilities. The ritual follows the pattern of the normal purification offering except, in these cases, a grain offering is permissible (vv. 11-13). The absence of blood in this ritual is problematic. The result, however, is the same — the priest ritually brings about expiation *(kipper)* and forgiveness *(nislah;* v. 13).

The Reparation Offering (5:14–6:7 [Heb. 5:14-26])

Because the reparation offering *('asham),* often translated as "the guilt offering," has similarities with the purification offering, it has occasionally been viewed as a type of the latter. For example, both are concerned with doing things that "ought not be done" and with "guilt" (cf. 4:3, 13, 22, 27; 5:17, 19; 6:4-7). The specific cases presented for the reparation offering, the distinct conceptual categories operative in this material, and the structure of the text all suggest, however, that the two offerings are distinct.

The reparation offering is required in matters relating to "trespass" *(ma'al)* against Yahweh. Trespass refers to "breaking faith" with Yahweh so that one's actions disturb or violate the realm of the holy. This is distinct from impurity, which requires a purification offering. Trespass is an offense against Yahweh that crosses over and violates the boundaries that set apart the holy things of Yahweh. It is a misappropriation or misuse of sancta (Milgrom

1991, 320-26). Trespass is an act of faithlessness within the Yahweh-Israel relationship. The person violates the trust that is essential to the relationship. Reparation for the sancta must be made and appropriate ritual activity must be enacted in order for the offender to obtain forgiveness.

The texts emphasize the situations that require the presentation of the reparation offering rather than the details of the ritual process itself (7:7-10 discusses the ritual process). The material is divided into two speeches, each one introduced by "Yahweh spoke to Moses" (5:14; 6:1 [Heb. 5:20]). The first speech presents two cases: 5:15-16 and 5:17-19. Each case includes a statement identifying the actions that generate guilt along with the necessary reparation that must be made. The second speech (6:1-7 [Heb. 5:20-26]) contains only one case, but with three distinct possibilities. It includes a statement concerning the reparation that must be made.

First Speech (5:14-19)
First Case (vv. 14-16): A person commits a trespass *(ma'al)* and sins unintentionally *(wehat'ah bishgagah)* in relation to the holy things of Yahweh *(miqqodsi yahweh)* (v. 14). Three key elements need discussion: trespass, unintentionally, and the holy things of Yahweh. In this case, the trespass is identified specifically as an act against (the misuse of) "the holy things of (dedicated to) Yahweh." Such items include, although are not limited to, land, clothing, animals, and the meat of certain sacrifices. A person appropriates an item dedicated to Yahweh and uses or consumes it inappropriately. Such a faithless act against Yahweh is subject to severe punishment, and the trespass must be "inadvertent" (see ch. 4) for a reparation offering to be effective, that is, the person does not know that a particular item is holy or dedicated and appropriates it without knowledge of its status or without malicious intention.

In order to make reparation, the person must bring a ram without blemish, convertible into silver in terms of the sanctuary shekel, as a reparation offering, make restitution for the holy thing, and add an additional one-fifth of the value of the violated sancta. The phrase "convertible into silver in terms of the sanctuary shekel" (v. 15) is problematic. Early in the history of the reparation offering, it was possible to present the monetary equivalent of an animal without actually slaughtering the animal. The priestly traditions believe the actual sacrifice is necessary: "the priest will perform the expiation ritual on your behalf with the ram of reparation offering, and you will be forgiven" (v. 16). Reparation and forgiveness require both the restoration of the violated sancta and the enactment of the ritual.

Second Case (vv. 17-19): The second case concerns a person who commits a sin but does not know it (v. 17; cf. 4:2), and who begins to feel guilty *('asham)*. This particular case involves suspected trespass (see Milgrom 1991, 339-45). The individual feels that a wrongful act has been committed and suspects a violation of sancta. In that the act is only suspected, it was inadvertent. Guilt, however, is present. The individual feels it, and if indeed the person has trespassed, guilt has been incurred. A ram is to be brought, monetary restitution made, and the reparation ritual enacted. The result is forgiveness.

Second Speech (6:1-7 [Heb. 5:20-26])

The second speech discusses the ways in which improper actions against other human beings constitute trespass against Yahweh. That one has "sworn falsely" is the common issue in these cases (vv. 3 [22], 5 [24]). In Israel, oaths were made in the context of the sacred. To swear falsely violates the sacred and breaks faith with Yahweh. It makes Yahweh a partner in malicious dishonesty. One trespasses on (i.e., misappropriates for dishonest use) Yahweh's honor and faithfulness.

There are three major cases. The first one has three subdivisions. The examples are representative — "and that person swears falsely with regard to *any* of the various things that a person may do to sin in this way" (v. 3 [22]; see also v. 7 [26]). The first situation concerns the deception of a neighbor in a matter of (a) deposit, (b) something held in pledge, or (c) robbery (v. 2a [21a]). The second case involves fraud by withholding something that is due another person (v. 2b [21b]). The third situation concerns finding something that has been lost and lying about it (v. 3a [22a]; cf. 19:11-13).

These cases agree that a wrong has been done and perpetuated through an oath sworn falsely. This creates a problem: How can sacrificial ritual address such flagrant sin? Milgrom argues that *confession* reduces such flagrant sin to an inadvertent sin, which can be forgiven through ritual enactment (1991, 373-78). The offender feels guilt and wants to make restoration (v. 4 [23]).

In the priestly traditions, four texts call for confession. (1) In Lev. 5:1-6, confession is required for four different forms of offense. Of these four, two clearly have to do with "sacred words": refusal to testify in the context of a public call for testimony and the utterance of a rash oath. (2) In Lev. 16:21, the annual ritual for community purification, the high priest confesses the sins of the people and places them on the head of the goat for Azazel. (3) In Lev. 26:40, a parenetic speech, the people's confession causes Yahweh to remember the promises to the ancestors in the context of treacherous sins. (4) In Num. 5:6-7, a connection is made between breaking faith with Yahweh, the feeling of guilt, and confession. In this case, confession means recognizing and accepting that one's actions have wronged other persons, and thus one has broken faith with Yahweh. Confession is placed within the context of ritual; it is ritualized confession. This sharpens its significance. Confession takes place within the context of the sacred and in the presence of Yahweh. The person actualizes the contrition of the heart in the ritual enactment of confession.

Several of the situations that call for confession have to do with false words spoken in a sacred context. Confession must also be placed in the context of sacred speech. In the priestly traditions, confession is required to set right acts of false speech associated with vows and oaths. In the context of the sacred, words have power: power to offend and power to amend. Confession functions to create a ritual context in which intentional sins can be ritually addressed (6:7 [5:26]).

The outcome of the ritual process is impressive: freedom from both incurred guilt and the feeling of guilt, expiation of sin, and divine forgiveness. The whole ritual process — a feeling of remorse, confession, restitution, sacrifice — creates a new state of existence. Ritual provides a context for people to address the problems associated with broken and faithless actions against

Yahweh and against other persons. It restores relations, sets matters aright, and provides a renewed context for life.

SECOND SERIES (6:8–7:38 [HEB. 6:1–7:38])

The Burnt Offering (6:8-13 [Heb. 6:1-6])

These instructions are aimed primarily at the priesthood (vv. 8-9a) and are concerned with "the torah of the burnt offering" *(torat ha'olah)*. In this context, "torah" refers to instructions concerning ritual procedures. The instructions specify how the priests are to clean the ashes from the altar, while maintaining the altar fire. The altar fire was believed to have originated with Yahweh (9:22-24), and the "divine" fire must be kept burning continuously (although this is not stated in ch. 6 in that the events of ch. 9 have not yet been narrated!).

These instructions are related to the *tamid* sacrifices, the burnt offerings presented each morning and each evening (see Exod. 29:38-46; Num. 28:3-8). The *tamid* sacrifices must be contextualized within priestly creation theology. The construction of the day is the foundational act of creation (Gen. 1:3-5). The daily morning and evening sacrifices function, in part, to mark out this creative moment. In this way, these sacrifices function to maintain the divinely constructed order and provide one means for Israel to participate in the ongoing order of creation and creative activity of God (Gorman 1990, 215-27).

The instructions concerning these sacrifices provide a larger theological context (Exod. 29:38-46). They are related to the divine presence that dwells in the midst of Israel, the Exodus from Egypt, and the priestly covenant with Abraham (see Gen. 17:7-8). An important theological relationship is established between divine presence, the story of promise, the history of redemption, and ritual enactment! In the priestly traditions, ritual is the primary way in which Israel relates to and interacts with the God who brought the nation out of bondage in order to dwell in its midst! This God is also the creator. Ritual, history, creation, and divine presence come together in the story of God and Israel bound together in relational life.

The primary concern of Lev. 6:8-13 [6:1-6] is to explain how the priests are to clean the ashes from the altar and, at the same time, keep the fire burning. This is emphasized three times (vv. 9 [2], 12 [5], 13 [6]). The issue is introduced in conjunction with the statement that the burnt offering is to remain on the altar through the night (v. 13 [6]). The text opens with a torah statement (v. 9 [2]), provides specific instructions for the disposal of the ashes (vv. 10-11 [3-4]) and the morning sacrifice (v. 12 [5]), and concludes with a restatement of the torah (v. 13 [6]).

In the morning, the priest puts on his priestly linen garments and removes the ashes from the altar. He then puts on common clothes and carries the ashes outside the camp to a clean place. After the cleaning process is completed, the priest puts more wood on the altar and begins the sacrifices of the day. Through the whole process, the altar fire must never go out.

The ashes are to be taken to "a clean place outside the camp" (this phrase is found elsewhere in Num. 19:9; Lev. 14:40, 41, 45 speak of "an unclean place" outside the camp). A place was set apart for this type of material, that is, material that was burned on the altar and, thereby, dedicated to God. Such material cannot remain in the camp. A pragmatic concern is also operative: the ashes cannot be allowed to pile up on the altar.

The Grain Offering (6:14-23 [Heb. 6:7-16])

This unit consists of two sections: vv. 14-18 [7-11] provide instruction *(torah)* for the grain offering *(minha)* and vv. 19-23 [12-16] focus on the special grain offering to be presented by the priests (see ch. 2 for a more detailed discussion of the grain offering). All the priests may eat the unleavened cakes (vv. 16a [9a], 18a [11a]) in a holy place (16b [9b]) after the memorial portion is offered. The cakes cannot safely be taken outside the tent area because they are most holy (v. 17b [10b]). Although the priestly portion is clearly a form of payment for priestly services, the eating itself takes on ritual nuances. Yahweh gives the grain offerings to the priests because they function as mediators. They exist and function in a realm that is betwixt and between the holy God and the sinful community (see the discussion of ch. 8). As priests, they are an embodiment of the holy to the people and, at the same time, an embodiment of the people to the holy. They consume the allotted portions as their due.

The priestly traditions emphasize the holiness of God — God is set apart in the most holy place — and recognize the need for sacred mediators; yet, at the same time, the divine presence in the midst of the people reflects an image of an egalitarian community with the sacred at its center. Ritual enactment seeks to locate the self and the community in a dynamic relationship with the divine. Mediators are required to go between God and the community.

The phrase, "anything that touches them shall be holy" (v. 18 [11]) occurs in only three other places: Lev. 6:27 [6:20] with reference to the purification offering; Exod. 29:37 with reference to the altar; and Exod. 30:26-29 with reference to items anointed with the holy anointing oil. Haran argues that holiness is a powerful force that is communicated to persons who touch these holy items (1978, 175-88). The evidence does not generally support such contagious holiness (although there may be exceptions), and it is doubtful that persons who touch these items would be given over to Yahweh. Levine argues that the primary issue is the verb "be/become holy," so that the statement means "anyone who is to touch these must be in a holy state" (1989, 37-38). The statement then functions to limit those who might come into contact with these items. Finally, Milgrom argues that the priestly traditions deny that persons can become holy through such contact, and he translates the text "whatever touches them shall become holy." The phrase refers to objects and not to persons (1991, 445-56). At the present time, the precise meaning remains uncertain.

Verses 19-23 [12-16] discuss the grain offering that Aaron is to offer on the day of his ordination. It is termed a "daily" or "regular" *(tamid)* grain offering! It consists of one-tenth of an ephah of choice flour, which is to be made with oil on a griddle. Half of it is to be offered in the morning and half of it is to be offered in the evening in order to provide a soothing fragrance for Yahweh. The anointed priests who succeed Aaron are to do the same thing. It is a perpetual due that must be offered to Yahweh.

This offering is not discussed in either of the texts that pre-scribe/describe the ritual of ordination for the priesthood (see Exod. 29 and Lev. 8–9). It is possible to understand this as a "regular" grain offering that was offered by newly anointed high priests on the day of their anointing, but it is doubtful that this would be called a *tamid*. The present text may prescribe the grain offering associated with the daily burnt offerings (see Exod. 29:38-41 and Num. 28:3-6). It is not identified as such in this text, however, and if it is a reference to regular grain offerings associated with the daily burnt offerings, it is certainly out of place. Thus, it is best understood as a separate grain offering offered by the high priest that began on the day of Aaron's anointing and was to continue everyday thereafter.

The passage concludes with a prohibition: the grain offerings of the priests are not to be eaten; they are to be wholly burned (v. 23 [16]). This offering contributes to the ritual construction of the priestly status and is not to be consumed by the priests. They receive portions from the sacrifices and offerings of the people as their rightful payment. The sacrifices and offerings that function to locate them in their priestly status belong entirely to Yahweh. The daily grain offering is a maintenance ritual that functions to mark out, recognize, and maintain the office of the anointed priest.

The Purification Offering (6:24-30 [6:17-23])

These verses discuss issues relating to the purification offering (see 4:1–5:13): the place of slaughter, its most holy status, a directive concerning where it is to be eaten, instructions on how to cleanse objects touched by its blood, a list of persons who may eat of this sacrifice, and a directive to burn the remains of an animal whose blood was brought inside the tent. The instructions are directed specifically to the priests and focus on their role in administering and watching over the sacrifices and offerings. In particular, the text discusses implications of the most holy status of the sacrifice.

The blood of the purification sacrifice communicates holiness to objects, and such objects must be either cleansed or destroyed.

Cloth can be washed in a holy place. Earthen vessels must be destroyed, whereas bronze vessels may be scoured and rinsed. This refers to the pots in which the meat would have been boiled (vv. 27-28 [20-21]).

The Reparation Offering (7:1-6)

These verses present instruction *(torah)* concerning the ritual of the reparation offering (see 5:14-26, where ritual instructions were not provided). The structure of the ritual is very similar to that of the purification offering: presentation, slaughter and blood manipulation, the burning of the fat, and the priestly consumption of the meat. The larger ritual process for reparation includes restoration *and* compensation. The sacrificial offering serves an expiatory purpose (see 5:16, 18), but restoration and compensation are essential to this process. The remainder of the text consists of instructions for the priests. The reparation offering is "most holy," and its meat may be eaten by all eligible priests in a holy place.

The Priestly Portions (7:7-10)

The statement that all the priests may eat of the reparation offering (7:6) explains the location of the present unit. It provides instruction for the priestly portions of the sacrifices. There are four primary concerns. (1) The ritual of the reparation offering is the same as that of the purification offering, and its proceeds go to the officiating priest (v. 7). (2) The priest who performs the ritual of the burnt offering receives the skin of the animal (v. 8). (3) Every grain offering that is prepared in an oven, in a pan, or on a griddle belongs to the priest who officiates at its ritual presentation (v. 9). (4) The uncooked grain offerings, either mixed with oil or dry, belong to all the priests (v. 10).

Further Instructions (7:11-38)

This material consists of four sets of instructions (vv. 11-18; 19-21; 22-27; 28-36) and a concluding summary statement (vv.

37-38). The instructions attempt to clarify what is appropriate and inappropriate consumption of sacrificial materials. The first unit defines the appropriate time frame for eating the sacrifices of well-being (vv. 11-18). The second unit prohibits the eating of sacrificial materials while in a state of uncleanness (vv. 19-21). The third unit prohibits eating the fat or blood of an animal (vv. 22-27). The fourth unit specifies those portions of the well-being sacrifice that are to go to the priests (vv. 28-36). The *karet* penalty (that person will be "cut off") occurs four times: in reference to those who eat the well-being sacrifices while unclean (v. 20, 21); in reference to those who eat the fat of an animal (v. 25); and in reference to those who eat the blood of an animal (v. 27).

7:11-18: This unit, focusing on the well-being offering (*zebah shelamim;* see ch. 3), consists of two parts: (1) the thanksgiving offering (*todah;* vv. 12-15); (2) the votive offering *(neder)* and freewill offering (*nedabah;* vv. 16-18). Each part specifies the time frame within which these sacrifices must be eaten.

The thanksgiving offering must include a grain offering of unleavened cakes mixed with oil, unleavened wafers spread with oil, cakes of choice flour soaked with oil (v. 12), and leavened cakes (v. 13). The officiating priest receives one cake of each kind (v. 14). The offerer must eat the thanksgiving offering on the day it is offered; none of it shall be eaten on the following day (v. 15).

The offerer may eat the votive or freewill offerings on the day they are offered and on the following day. On the third day, what is left must be burned (vv. 16-17). If any of the flesh is eaten on the third day, the sacrifice is not acceptable and the offerer will not receive the benefits of the sacrifice. Improper eating of the sacrificial meat is considered an abomination, and the one who eats must bear the punishment associated with this action (v. 18). The phrase "to bear the guilt/punishment" emphasizes that offenders will not escape the consequences of their actions.

The precise reason for the different time frames is not clear. It may be related to the different reasons for these offerings. A thank offering is a response to an experience of divine grace in life, a response to the goodness of Yahweh actually experienced. The votive and freewill offerings originate in the will of the offerer who chooses to present them. In the case of the votive offering, the offerer makes a vow without necessarily first experiencing divine grace. If true, this would suggest a carefully nuanced understanding of the divine-human relationship as it is worked out, experienced, and enacted in the common and mundane situations of life.

The consumption of the animal is part of the larger ritual process. The concluding prohibition indicates that improper eating can invalidate the effectiveness of the sacrifice. The offerer experiences the reality of the divine-human relationship in the meal. Such eating infuses the common and the everyday with the sacred and places them in the context of the sacred. At the same time, it brings the sacred into the context of the common and the everyday. It is an enacted and embodied experience of communion.

7:19-21: This unit prohibits the eating of sacrificial food by an unclean person. It opens with a prohibition against the eating of flesh that touches any unclean thing (v. 19a). Such contact makes the flesh unclean. Unclean flesh must be burned, whereas all other flesh may be eaten by anyone who is clean (19b). Both the flesh and the person who eats it must be clean. Anyone who eats sacrificial meat while in an unclean state shall be cut off *(karet)* from his or her people (v. 20). The warning is restated in v. 21.

The *karet* penalty is the strongest threat available. It is the consequence of acts that violate the sacred order of the Israelite community and blur the distinctions between the sacred and the profane (Frymer-Kensky 1983, 404). It is specifically called for when a person (1) neglects certain ritual duties (Gen. 17:14; Num. 19:13, 20); (2) undertakes prohibited worship (Lev. 17:4, 9; 20:2-6; (3) undertakes certain prohibited activities (Lev. 18:29; Num. 15:30-31); and (4) undertakes improper ritual activity (Exod. 12:15, 19; 30:33, 38; 31:14; Lev. 7:20-21, 25, 27; 17:10, 14; 23:29, 30). The *karet* penalty is punishment by God, not the community (the distinction is clear in Lev. 20:2-5). The punishment comes through the extermination or extirpation of one's lineage (see Wold 1979; Milgrom 1990, 405-8). The priestly traditions draw a distinction between the death penalty as community punishment and the extermination of one's lineage as divine punishment. The *karet* penalty involves the latter.

7:22-27: These prohibitions are intended for the whole community (v. 22-23a). The first prohibits eating the fat of sacrificial animals (an ox, a sheep, or a goat; vv. 23b-25) or animals that have died or been killed in the wild (v. 24). Any person who eats the fat of a sacrificial animal shall be cut off (*karet;* v. 25). Although the specific context of this statement is the well-being offering, the text actually prohibits the fat of *any* animal that may be offered in fire to Yahweh. Thus, it includes the purification offerings of which the priests must eat (see 6:26 [6:19]).

The second prohibits eating of the blood of any animal (vv. 26-27). This prohibition is also followed by the *karet* penalty. The fat and the blood belong to Yahweh and have specific uses in the ritual process (see 3:16b-17 and ch. 17). They are not available for human consumption.

7:28-36: This unit focuses on the parts of the well-being offerings that belong to the priests, and it is directed at the whole Israelite community (vv. 28-29a). The one who is making the offering must bring it personally and present it (hand it over) to the priest (vv. 29b-30). The fat is to be turned into smoke on the altar, whereas the breast, after it is raised in presentation and dedication to Yahweh, belongs to the priest (v. 31).

In addition, the right thigh of the well-being sacrifice goes to the priest, who manipulates the sacrificial blood (vv. 32-33). Both the breast and the thigh of the well-being sacrifice belong to the priests as their perpetual due (v. 34). Only those, however, who have been brought forward (installed) as priests may eat of them (see 6:14-18 [6:7-11] for a discussion of the priestly benefits).

Concluding Statement (7:37-38)

Although these verses initially functioned as a conclusion only to chs. 6–7, they now function as a conclusion to the whole discussion of sacrifice in chs. 1–7. They are in tension with 1:1, which locates the giving of the instructions for sacrifice in the context of the tent of meeting. Although this tension reflects uneven editing and redaction of the material, it provides an important clue for understanding these materials. It is not necessary to resolve all of the problems and tensions. Certainly the problems are of importance in any effort to reconstruct the history of the text or the history of Israelite religion. Part of that reconstruction, however, must recognize that the priestly traditionists were willing to create and pass along texts with such problems and tensions firmly embedded within them. This suggests that for all of their attention to detail, the priests maintained a certain redactional freedom in constructing texts.

ORDINATION, FOUNDING, AND TRAGEDY
Leviticus 8–10

Leviticus 8–10 move in two directions. First, they narrate the ordination of the priesthood and the inauguration of the tabernacle cult. In this way, they conclude the "story" of the construction of the divine dwelling place, which is, at the same time, the sacred place of sacrifice. Second, they tell the story of Aaron's two sons who brought "strange fire" into the holy place and were killed by fire from Yahweh — on the very day of the ordination and founding! In this way, they anticipate the instructions on purity and impurity in chs. 11–15 and the instructions for the annual day of purification in ch. 16. The glory of the newly inaugurated tabernacle cult, marked by the fire of Yahweh consuming the sacrifices and offerings, is juxtaposed with the horror of the forbidden priestly act, marked by the fire of Yahweh "consuming" the two sons of Aaron. Life and death are at stake in this story of divine presence and human community. The priests are ritually located in a dangerous place and are called to undertake dangerous activity!

ORDINATION AND FOUNDING (8–9)

Leviticus 8–9 are best understood as two interrelated parts within a larger ritual and narrative context. Leviticus 8 narrates the ritual of the ordination of the priesthood and the ritual founding of holy space, whereas ch. 9 narrates the founding and inauguration of the tabernacle cult as the newly ordained priesthood presents the sacrifices and offerings for the first time. Ritual enactment and narrative depiction are intertwined and fused. Although the ritual processes are central, they are narratively contextualized within the story of the inauguration of the tabernacle cult. Hence, chs. 8–9 depict narratively and enact ritually the ordination of the priesthood and the founding of the tabernacle cult, both of which are parts of the same process.

These texts do not reflect or serve as a basis for repeated and regular rituals in Israel. These are one-time ritual occasions, ritual acts of founding. Israel, in all likelihood, knew rituals that were similar and related to these, for example, a regular ritual of ordination for priests (see 7:35, "when they have been brought forward to serve Yahweh as priests"), but the exact ritual processes of chs. 8–9 will not again be enacted.

Leviticus 8 reflects the structure and movement of a rite of passage (Gorman 1990, 115-39). Such rituals function to move a person or group from one status into another status. In this case, Aaron and his sons begin the ritual as "lay" persons, and the ritual moves them into and locates them in their priestly, institutional status.

Leviticus 8 looks back to Yahweh's instructions for the ritual in Exod. 29. The chapters contain differences in details that suggest distinct tradition processes, although the present form of the text clearly views Lev. 8 as the enactment of the instructions in Exod. 29. This is indicated by the repeated use of the phrase, "and Moses did just as Yahweh commanded him" (vv. 4a, 9b, 13b, 17b, 21b, 29b, 36 [slightly modified]). Indeed, this formula functions as a structural device in the text. Precise obedience to Yahweh's commandments is central to this text *and* the ritual depicted in it. The phrase occurs seven times and links this text to other texts of founding, in which a sevenfold structure is exhibited (see Blenkinsopp 1976; and the Introduction).

Leviticus 9 does not use the "obedience-execution" formula, although it does structure the narration of the ritual proper into seven distinct segments: the purification offering for Aaron (vv. 8-11); the burnt offering for Aaron (vv. 12-14); the purification offering for the people (v. 15); the burnt offerings for the people (v. 16); the cereal offering (v. 17); the well-being offering (vv. 18-21); and Aaron's initial blessing of the people (v. 22). The seven-part "structure" of these two rituals not only connects them to each other, it also relates them to Gen. 1. The construction and inauguration of the tabernacle cult are part of the ongoing creative activity of God shared with the community. The priestly blessing of the people (Lev. 9:22) reflects the divine blessing of human beings (Gen. 1:28). Following the priestly blessing, the fire of Yahweh comes forth and consumes the sacrifices and offerings on the altar. The tabernacle cult has been founded; Yahweh is indeed present in the midst of Israel!

The Ordination of the Priesthood (ch. 8)

Introduction (vv. 1-4)

The ordination of the priesthood, a ritual of founding, is to be enacted at the entrance of the tent and in the presence of the whole community. The community is present as audience-participant. The ordination of the priesthood takes place at the door of the tent because this is the primary space in which the priesthood will undertake its duties. The priests are ritually located in their institutional status in the very place in which they will execute their priestly duties. At the same time, this ritual must be enacted within the context of the gathered community. The priesthood is a social institution and must be instituted, constructed, contextualized, and located within larger social and institutional structures (see Nelson 1993, 39-53).

The Ritual Proper (vv. 5-30)

Washing and Clothing (vv. 6-9): Aaron and his sons are ritually washed by Moses (v. 6). This washing serves two purposes. First, it "marks" them as the ones on whom the ritual will have its effects. These are the persons who are being moved from one status to another. Second, the washing ritually cleanses Aaron and his sons. Ritual purity is necessary for ritual movement into the priestly status.

It is important to note that they are not washed again at the end of the ritual (cf. Lev. 16:4, 24). This ritual moves the priests into a permanent ritual status. The priesthood is understood as a permanent institutional position — the priests are the ones who stand between Yahweh and the people, the holy and the common, the sacred and the profane, the clean and the unclean.

Moses then clothes Aaron in the special high priestly garments (vv. 7-9; see Exod. 28 for the construction of these garments). The materials and working of these vestments reflect various parts and aspects of the tabernacle (see Haran 1978, 165-74). Clothing functions to merge space and status, person and place. Aaron's clothing connects him to the tabernacle area and locates him in his institutional status. Equally important, however, is the ritual act of clothing a person. The clothing serves to mark off Aaron's special status as the high priest. This is a moment of ritual "enclothement" when Aaron "puts on" the role of high priest. These garments distinguish him from the other priests who are not clothed at this time. The priesthood has distinct categories within it, and the ordination ritual seeks to mark out these distinctions.

The Anointing and Clothing (vv. 10-13): Moses takes the holy anointing oil (see Exod. 30:22-33 for the composition of this oil) and anoints (1) the tabernacle and its contents (v. 10); (2) the altar and items associated with it (v. 11); and (3) Aaron himself (v. 12). The purpose of the anointing is "to make holy" *(leqaddesh)* the objects and persons on which the oil is placed. Hence, the tabernacle and its associated cultic objects, the altar and its associated utensils, and Aaron are all anointed and made holy. Their common anointing functions to place them in a common status. Aaron's status and the "space" he occupies are ritually constructed at the same time and in the same way. Although different words are used for the actual act — the tabernacle is "anointed," the altar is "sprinkled," Aaron has it "poured" on him — the purpose is the same, to make holy.

This is a crucial moment in the larger priestly story. The tabernacle, altar, and high priest are made holy through ritual enactment. The "holy" is a shared construction of Yahweh and Israel. On the one hand, the tabernacle is holy because Yahweh is present in it; on the other hand, the tabernacle is holy because of ritual enactment. The convergence of the divine story and the human story is reflected in this dual understanding of "making holy."

Moses then clothes Aaron's sons. Ritual enclothement marks off and emphasizes identity, so the enclothement of the high priest must be separated from the enclothement of the rest of the priests.

The Purification Offering (vv. 14-17): This is the first presentation of a purification offering on the tabernacle altar. Moses serves as priest in this ritual, although his role transcends that of priest. Moses is the inaugurator of the cult, and, as such, he stands outside of the normal limiting categories of priest, prophet, or even king (see Gorman 1990, 141-49). He is able to cross boundaries that are dangerous and carefully guarded (e.g., in Exod. 24:15-18 he enters into the divine glory visible on Mt. Sinai). The initial presentation of the sacrifices and offerings requires someone who stands outside the normal structures of society (the priesthood, it must be remembered, is not yet established).

At the same time, Moses demonstrates how the sacrificial rites are to be enacted. It is common in rites of passage for the initiates to receive instructions concerning their future status. A similar instructional moment is found in the wilderness traditions. Sinai stands at the center of this passage from slavery to freedom and functions as a place of instruction for the people (see Cohn 1981, 7-23).

This text narrates the first presentation of the purification offering and provides a clear explanation for the actions associated with the blood. The blood on the horns of the altar functions to purify the altar, and the blood poured out at the base of the altar functions to make it holy (v. 15; see the extended discussion in Lev. 4). If the altar has become defiled, it has, at the same time, lost its holy status. Thus, if the altar must be purified, it must also be reconsecrated. Both actions are necessary in order to restore it to its proper and appropriate status.

The Ram of the Burnt Offering (vv. 18-21): The burnt offering functions in its normal way (see ch. 1). In that this is a founding ritual, the presentation of the burnt offering serves as a model and paradigm — this is the way it is to be done.

The Ram of Ordination (vv. 22-29): The ram of ordination is central to this ritual and is found in no other ritual. In relation to the priests, "ordination" *(millu'im)* is understood as "filling the hand" and points to their role as the ones who "fill their hands" with the sacrifices presented to Yahweh. They receive the sacrifices and offerings from the hand of the people and present them to Yahweh. Although it does have conceptual and ritual similarities with the well-being sacrifices, the manipulation of the blood of the ordination sacrifice is distinct.

Moses places some of the blood on the right earlobe, the right thumb, and the right big toe of Aaron and his sons and then throws the rest of it on all sides of the altar. Elsewhere, the blood is used in this way only in the ritual restoration for a person recovered from a defiling skin eruption (see 14:1-32). The latter ritual also includes materials used in the preparation of water for cleansing corpse-defiled persons (Num. 19). These three rituals share a concern for death. Some type of contact with the realm of death has taken place and a seven-day ritual process is required in order to relocate those involved in the realm of life. Numbers 19 provides instructions for the ritual production of water for cleansing a person contaminated by a corpse. A red cow is taken outside the camp, presented to the priest, and slaughtered. The priest, identified as Eleazer, sprinkles some of its blood seven times toward the entrance of the tent of meeting. The skin, flesh, blood, and dung are then burned along with cedarwood, red material, and hyssop (Lev. 14:6 includes the last three items). The ashes of the cow are mixed with water, and, on the third and seventh days of a seven-day ritual process, the water is sprinkled on the contaminated person to effect purification. It is the blood of the cow that functions to purify. At the same time, the life of the animal in the blood functions to move the person from the realm of death to life. The blood both purifies and restores!

The priestly traditionists view skin diseases as eruptions of the realm of death. This is indicated in Numbers 12 when Miriam becomes covered with a skin disease *(metsora'at)* and Aaron asks that she not be like one born dead (vv. 10-12; see Feldman 1977, 37-41). Unclean skin diseases were associated with the decay and rot of death, the eating and wasting away of the person, and they placed a person in contact with the realm of death (see Lev. 13). The person with an unclean skin disease graphically "bodies forth" the realm of death. In the seven-day ritual for the person who has recovered, the blood of the reparation offering is placed on the person's extremities (14:14, 25). The blood purifies, but it also restores the person to the realm of life. The blood, as ritual agent, holds together the realm of death, from which the person is moving (in the death of the animal), and the realm of life, into which the person is moving (in the life that is in the blood). This ritual is designed to relocate the person within the ordinary, everyday contexts of life.

The priestly ordination also reflects this movement from death to life. The key to this is found in Num. 16–17. A series of rebellions against Moses and Aaron, especially over the issue of the priesthood, result in the establishment of Aaron and his house as the rightful priests. Numbers 16:1-40 [Heb. 16:1–17:5] narrates that Korah, Kohath, Dathan, and Abiram accused Moses and Aaron of exalting themselves above the rest of the people. The accusation raises questions concerning who is holy and who can approach God in the sacred area (Num. 16:4-11). The glory of Yahweh appears to decide the dispute, and the leaders of the rebellion along with their households are swallowed up by the earth. Fire comes forth from Yahweh and consumes their followers. The censers that had been used by the rebels to burn incense become holy through their contact with the fire of Yahweh, and they are hammered as a cover on the altar. Both the narrative and the censers hammered on the altar are to serve as reminders that it is dangerous to enter into the realm of the holy without appropriate authorization from Yahweh.

The following day, the whole congregation rebels against Moses and Aaron accusing them of killing the people (Num. 16:41-50 [Heb. 17:6-15]). The anger of Yahweh again breaks out against the people in the form of a plague. Moses instructs Aaron to put fire from the altar and incense in his censer in order to effect expiation *(kipper)* on behalf of the people. The text states that Aaron "stood between the dead and the living; and the plague was stopped" (6:48 [Heb. 7:13]). Aaron stands between the people and Yahweh, between the dead and the living, in order to effect expiation.

Finally, Num. 17:1-13 [Heb. 17:16-28] narrates the selection of Aaron's family to be priests. The response of the people to the selection is crucial for understanding the priestly ordination ritual: "The children of Israel said to Moses, 'We are perishing; we are dying! All of us are dying! Every person who dares to approach the tabernacle of Yahweh will surely die! Is it the case that all of us are to perish?'" (Num. 17:12-13 [Heb. 17:27-28]). The answer is "no" because the sons of Aaron have been placed in the tabernacle to perform the sacred, ritual duties. The priesthood stands in a dangerous place — it is located in a ritual space that moves between life and death. The ordination ritual locates them in a place that exists at the intersection of life and death.

Further Use of the Anointing Oil (v. 30): Moses next takes some of the anointing oil and some of the blood that is on the altar and sprinkles this mixture on Aaron and his vestments and on Aaron's sons and their vestments. The anointing oil, as already noted, functions to make holy the persons and objects on which it is placed. The blood functions to connect the priests materially to the altar and indicates their special relationship both to the sacrificial blood and the altar. These are the ones who are to manipulate the blood on the altar. The parallel anointing of Aaron and his sons indicates their shared status.

Final Instructions to the Priests (vv. 31-36)

The final instructions consist of three main elements: (1) instructions regarding the consumption of the sacrifices and offerings (vv. 31-32); (2) a temporal note concerning the ordination process (vv. 33-35); and (3) a note that things were done just as Yahweh commanded (v. 36).

The priests are instructed to boil the sacrificial meat at the entrance of the tent of meeting and eat it there with the bread of ordination. What is not eaten must be burned. This is a paradigmatic enactment of the priestly consumption of the sacrifices and offerings in holy space — space and activity become merged!

The length of the ordination process is seven days. The priests are to remain at the entrance and keep the charge of Yahweh lest they die. The warning indicates that the priestly position is a dangerous position. The "charge" has to do with the instructions for their ordination process. It cannot refer at this point to specific priestly duties in that they are still in the process of becoming priests.

Leviticus 8 concludes with a statement that the ritual has conformed to Yahweh's instructions. The priesthood is now constructed and located within the institution of the tabernacle. They are now in a position to present the sacrifices and offerings in the context of and on behalf of the community.

The Inauguration of the Tabernacle Cult (ch. 9)

Leviticus 9 narrates the actual beginning of the *priestly* tabernacle cult. It tells the story of the first sacrifices and offerings presented by the newly ordained priesthood. The instructions in vv. 1-7 emphasize five points. First, the whole process must follow the instructions of Yahweh (vv. 6, 7). Second, the priests must enact the rituals at the entrance of the tent ("before Yahweh" in vv. 2-4 and "the entrance" in v. 5). Third, the ritual is to take place in the context of the gathered community (v. 5). Fourth, the stated purpose of this ritual is to effect expiation *(kipper)* for the whole community (v. 7). Fifth, the glory of Yahweh will appear in the sight of the whole community in conjunction with the priestly activity (v. 6).

Aaron presents the calf of the purification offering for himself (vv. 8-11). The procedure in this text does not follow exactly the specifications found in 4:3-12. The differences may be explained, in part, by recognizing the distinctive nature of this ritual as a founding ritual — this is the first time the high priest presents the sacrifices and offerings. The sacrifices "for Aaron" are most likely intended to include his sons, so that in this instance the purification offering is for the priesthood and not simply for the high priest. Aaron then offers the ram of the burnt offering for the priesthood (vv. 12-14). Thus the normative order is established: purification offering followed by burnt offering.

Aaron then presents the purification offering for the people (v. 15), the burnt offering for the people (v. 16), and the grain offering for the people (v. 17). Aaron turns the representative portion of the grain offering into smoke on the altar along with the morning burnt offering (v. 17). He then sacrifices the ox of the well-being offering for the people (vv. 18-21). Every detail complies with the divine instructions. A basic ritual order is established and actualized (see Haran 1961; Rainey 1970). This enactment becomes paradigmatic for priestly ritual order.

After the sacrifices and offerings have been presented, Aaron lifts his hands and blesses the people (v. 22). Moses and Aaron enter into the tent together, and, when they exit, they again bless the people (v. 23a). At this moment the glory of Yahweh appears to all the people, fire comes from the presence of Yahweh and consumes the materials on the altar, and the people shout and fall on their faces (vv. 23b-24). Yahweh has taken up residence in the tabernacle, confirmed the ordination of the priests, and accepted the sacrifices and offerings that they have placed on the altar. The fire that burns on the altar is the fire of Yahweh. The tabernacle cult is now operative: divine presence, sacred space, sacred persons, and sacred activities. Yahweh does indeed dwell in the midst of the community!

The Death of Nadab and Abihu (Ch. 10)

On the very day that the newly ordained priesthood presents the first sacrifices and offerings, Nadab and Abihu, two of Aaron's sons and two of the newly ordained priests, bring "strange fire" before Yahweh, with the consequence that fire comes out from Yahweh and kills them. This story provides graphic images of the very real danger that is associated with priestly activity in the holy place.

An interesting narrative pattern emerges. Just as the Israelites worshipped "other gods" immediately after entering into the Sinai covenant with God (Exod. 32), so now these two priests present "strange fire" to God immediately after the cult is made operational. These stories present narrative juxtaposition of construction and deconstruction, of actualization and disruption, of order and chaos. A similar dynamic and narrative unfolding is found in the opening chapters of Genesis. The image of Yahweh and humans dwelling together in the divinely constructed garden is quickly disrupted through human actions. The pattern of divine presence and human sin produces a variety of divine responses. The freedom of Yahweh to act within the context of the story is emphasized, although the stories agree that Yahweh does not act in a way that would bring the story to an end (cf. the flood story in Gen. 6–9; see Rendtorff 1989). The merging of story and ritual is clearly recognizable in Lev. 10. Ritualization and narrativization intertwine to image and "re-member" Israel's founding story. Narrative becomes a form of ritualization, whereas ritual becomes narrativized.

Leviticus 10 has three basic movements: (1) the initial problem (vv. 1-7); (2) divine instructions (vv. 8-15); and (3) conflict between Moses and Aaron (vv. 16-20). The problem caused by Nadab and Abihu provides the context for both the instructions (vv. 8-15) and the additional problems associated with the failure of the priests to eat the sacrifices (vv. 16-20). In addition, the problems raised here generate, in part, the need for the ritual of ch. 16.

The Death of Nadab and Abihu (vv. 1-7)

The death of Nadab and Abihu disrupts the celebration of the founding of the tabernacle cult. The anguish of the event is heightened precisely because it takes place on the very day that the divine fire had come forth from the tent. The discussion of Moses and Aaron concerning the disposal of the remains of the purification offering indicates that this is the eighth day of the ordination ritual. The ironic juxtaposition of images is startling: the fire that initially came forth and consumed the sacrifices and offerings is the same fire that now comes forth and "consumes" the two priests (cf. the language in 9:24 and 10:2).

The text states that Nadab and Abihu "offered 'strange fire' (*'esh zarah*) to Yahweh, such as Yahweh had not commanded them" (v. 1). Although the precise nature of the act is not certain, the resulting problem is obvious. The *words* of the text are crucial: "they presented strange fire to Yahweh." They have acted as priests — they put incense in their censers and burned it in the presence of Yahweh — but they have used fire that was not commanded. The holy cannot be violated by any outside or strange material. Such confusion of categories leads to pollution, defilement, and disruption of the holy place. Holy fire must come from within the realm of the holy, from the coals on the altar; it is fire that comes from Yahweh! As priests who intentionally offer "strange" fire, they must bear the punishment for their violation — death is the consequence.

Moses speaks to Aaron in an effort to explain and understand what has happened. "This is what Yahweh meant" (v. 3) clearly indicates that the death of the two priests exemplifies and actualizes what Yahweh had said concerning the priestly duty of maintaining the boundaries of the holy. The explanatory statement in v. 3 indicates that the whole community is to know the holiness and glory of God through the priests who draw near to Yahweh. The holiness of God and the glory of God are parallel phrases in this statement. In part, God's holiness and glory are made manifest (1) by a priesthood that functions within prescribed bounds and (2) by God's protection of the holy from improper intrusions. Failure to perform the priestly duties in an appropriate fashion forces God to act in order to preserve the holiness of the sacred area.

The tunics the men were wearing were used to drag their bodies outside the camp. The fire did not "consume" them in the sense that it burned them up completely. The fire killed them; their remains must be disposed of properly. Mishael and Elzaphan, sons of Uzziel the uncle of Aaron, were assigned the task. A question arises at this point: Do the two corpses in the tabernacle create impurity? It might be argued that their corpses were purified by the divine fire (cf. the censers of the rebels in Num. 16:36-38 [Heb. 17:1-3]). In that the bodies are pulled out by their clothing, it would appear that the corpses can defile. It is probable that this problem gives rise to the annual ritual of purification (Lev. 16). Although questions remain, the ritual of ch. 16 is clearly related to this event (see vv. 1-2).

Moses forbids Aaron and his sons Eleazar and Ithamar to mourn. The *people* may mourn the "burning that Yahweh has sent," but the anointed priests must remain at the entrance of the tent and refrain from participating in the mourning rites. Such mourning would align them too closely with the dead, who are both violators of the sacred and defiled (rules for the priests and funeral rites are specified in 21:1-4).

Instructions for the Priests (vv. 8-11)

Verses 8-11 contain two distinct instructional statements. First, the priests must refrain from strong drink or wine when entering the tent, lest they die (vv. 8-9). The effects of the drink might bring about a disruption of appropriate practices (and the narrator has just indicated the consequences of "strange behavior" in the holy place). The priests must have clear heads while performing their duties.

The second statement is central for a correct understanding of the priestly role, and it functions to set the stage for the instructions on purity and impurity (chs. 11–15). The priests are "to distinguish *(lahabdil)* between the holy and the common, and between the unclean and the clean, and to teach *(lehorot)* the children of Israel all the statutes that Yahweh has spoken to them through Moses" (v. 10). The word translated "distinguish" refers in Gen. 1 to God's acts of "separation" in creation (see e.g., vv. 4, 6, 7, 18). The priestly separation of ritual categories is significantly related to and, in a very real sense, continues the creative work of God. Thus, the instructions on purity and impurity constitute one aspect of the very good order of creation (see Gen. 1:31), and the priests are to watch over and maintain the basic categories — the holy and the common, the clean and the unclean. In addition, they are to teach (from "torah") the people the divine statutes. In this way the whole community is expected to participate in the ongoing process of observing and maintaining the order of creation.

Conflict Erupts (vv. 12-20)

Verses 12-20 focus on the priestly consumption of the sacrifices and offerings. The priests must eat the grain offerings in a holy place and the breast and the thigh of the elevation offering in a clean place. The latter are available to the whole priestly family (vv. 12-15). These offerings are the perpetual due of the priests.

A conflict now arises between Moses and Aaron (vv. 16-20). The remains of the goat of the purification offering for the people had been burned. This angers Moses because they should have been eaten by the priests "to remove the guilt of the community" (v. 17). In that the blood was not brought inside the tent, its meat should have been eaten (in conformity with 6:26, 30). In addition, the priestly consumption of the purification sacrifices plays a crucial role in the expiatory process — the eating functions to remove the guilt of the people.

This is an example of the priestly ability to "embody the impossible." The priests, who are holy, are to eat the "defiled" remains of the sacrificial animal. The impurity of the altar, on which the blood was thrown, has been absorbed and communicated to the remains. The holiness of the priests "consumes" the impurity of the remains — two radically opposed realms are merged. The priests are able to embody and hold together contradictory categories because they have been placed in a permanent ritual status in which they stand between the holy and the common. They enact the breakdown of normal order so as to generate a renewed and transformed order.

Aaron's response is not entirely clear. The intent seems to question whether this eating of the sacrifices would have changed the situation. The implied answer suggests that it would not have made any difference. This does not, however, fully address Moses' question: "Why did you not eat them as instructed?" Aaron argues that the events of the day made eating the purification offerings appear out of place, if not absolutely improper. The death of the priests created a situation that seemed to disqualify the purification offerings of that day. "Would it have been proper in the eyes of Yahweh?" (v. 19). In this way, Aaron demonstrates the priestly freedom to interpret the instructions in specific contexts! Yahweh's instructions provide frameworks for enactment!

INSTRUCTIONS ON PURITY
Leviticus 11–16

Leviticus 11–16 contain instructions on purity and impurity *(torot)* for a variety of situations (chs. 11–15) and prescriptions for the enactment of the annual day of purification (ch. 16). These instructions reflect a concern for sacred space and the life of the community lived in the presence of Yahweh. The ability to distinguish (to separate) between the clean and the unclean protects sacred space from possible defilement. The annual ritual functions to restore and maintain the integrity of sacred space and the camp.

The instructions of chs. 11–15 focus on the preservation of sacred space and the maintenance of purity within the life of the people: clean and unclean foods (ch. 11); purification of a woman after childbirth (ch. 12); identification of an unclean skin disease (ch. 13); purification from an unclean skin disease (ch. 14); and bodily discharges (ch. 15). Each set of instructions is concerned, to some degree, with bodily boundaries. The concern with *foods* has to do with the intake of materials into the body. *Childbirth* has to do with the generation of life in relation to the body of the woman. *Unclean skin diseases* focus on the integrity and well-being of the body. *Bodily discharges* reflect the concern for the integrity of the boundaries of the body, in particular, those parts of the body associated with fertility and the generation of life. The integrity of the community is reflected in the integrity of the body, and the boundaries of both must be carefully watched over and guarded.

These chapters certainly appear to be out of touch with the contemporary context. A theological understanding of these rules is not a call either (1) to incorporate these instructions into the contemporary situation or (2) to adapt these "body-sensitive" rules to the present context. They do, however, have something important to say to contemporary theology. These instructions take the body seriously. They recognize that theology must speak to and address persons who exist in terms of bodies, and that theological discourse must take the body seriously.

Western culture has generally devalued the body and denied its significance for understanding the self. Christian theology has often been guilty of communicating and generating a suspicion of the body that has created a sense of "dis-ease" with the body. These instructions suggest that a concern for the body is at the heart of theology and the practice of religion and that human physicality must be taken seriously for any adequate explanation of human life and existence.

Clean and Unclean Foods (Ch. 11)

Yahweh speaks these instructions to Moses and Aaron. This is the first time that Aaron is included as a recipient of the words of Yahweh, which reflects his assumption of the role of high priest (see ch. 9). The priestly duty to separate the holy from the common and the clean from the unclean (10:10-11) provides the immediate context.

The chapter addresses two separate but related issues: (1) the distinction between clean and unclean animals (vv. 2b-23, 41-45) and (2) the specification of animals whose carcasses can defile through contact (vv. 24-40). Verses 46-47 provide a final summary statement. The text reflects a variety of linguistic forms and structures.

Deuteronomy 14 closely parallels Lev. 11. A precise reconstruction of their development and relationship remains problematic. Although there are significant differences between the texts, their content is fundamentally the same. References to the Deuteronomic text will be minimal.

Clean and Unclean Animals (vv. 2b-23)

The opening unit identifies the characteristics of edible animals. The text discusses land animals (vv. 2b-8), water animals (vv.

9-12), animals of the air (vv. 13-19), and winged insects (vv. 20-23).

Land Animals (vv. 2b-8)

Following an introductory statement (v. 2b), this unit identifies the characteristics of animals that are edible (v. 3), specifies four animals that are forbidden (vv. 4-7), and concludes with a summary statement (v. 8). Two characteristics define a clean land animal: (1) it must have true hoofs that are cleft through, and (2) it must chew the cud. Recent discussions make it clear that the animal must have true hoofs that are cleft through the middle (Levine 1989, 66; Milgrom 1991, 646-47; Houston 1993, 36). This view makes sense of v. 26, which, otherwise, seems to contradict itself (i.e., animals that have hoofs, but without clefts through the middle, are unclean). Animals that chew the cud (ruminants) regurgitate their food for further chewing. Both criteria must be present to qualify the animal for consumption (Deut. 14:4-5 contains a list of such animals).

Verses 4-7 identify four disqualified animals. These are borderline cases that would have been available to the Israelites: the camel, the rock-badger, the hare, and the pig. The first three are excluded because, even though they chew the cud, they do not have hoofs that are divided down the middle. Only the pig is excluded because it does not chew the cud. In this text, all four have equal status as unclean foods.

Various theories have been offered to explain why these particular characteristics disqualify animals (for a review, see Houston 1993, 68-123). At present, no single theory explains all the evidence. A variety of ideological, social, and theological factors converge in these instructions (see Firmage 1990, 177-97; Houston 1993, 218-58).

First, the structure of Lev. 11 reflects, to a degree, the basic categories of creation: land, water, and air (see Douglas 1979, 53-56; Soler 1979). This suggests that the issue of edible animals is related to and contextualized within the basic categories of creation theology. Second, the primary domesticated animals in Israel — the ox, the goat, and the sheep — provide a basic pattern for acceptable and edible animals. Other animals are edible, but they must exhibit the characteristics found in domesticated animals. Third, animals associated with the altar and with the realm of the sacred contribute to the priestly construction of edible animals (see Firmage 1990, 194-97). Finally, animals are evaluated, at least in part, in terms of their primary means of locomotion (e.g., land animals should walk on all fours).

The "anomaly" plays a role in the exclusion of some animals. Anomalous animals do not clearly reflect socially and ritually constructed categories. Just as creation is divided into its basic categories (air, water, and land), so animals are located in their appropriate habitats (see Gen. 1:1–2:4a). Animals should reflect the norms associated with their particular location and habitat. These norms may include eating habits, means of locomotion, basic habits and conduct, and/or appearance. Failure to reflect the norms results in exclusion from the table. In addition, the human table must reflect the table of God (Firmage 1990, 194).

The concluding phrase emphasizes the importance of recognizing and observing the distinction between clean and unclean animals (v. 8). Unclean animals are not to be eaten, and their dead carcasses are not to be touched. To eat them or to touch their carcass creates impurity (purification processes for contact with their corpses are detailed in vv. 24-28, but no rite of purification is included for one who eats them).

Water Animals (vv. 9-12)

Verses 9-12 address issues relating to creatures of the water. Edible water creatures must have both fins and scales (v. 9). This unit includes a general statement concerning the excluded ones (v. 10), prohibits either eating or touching the carcasses of excluded ones (v. 11), and concludes with a summary statement (v. 12). No list of clean and unclean creatures is included.

The excluded animals are termed "detestable" (*sheqets;* cf. "unclean" [*tame'*] in vv. 2b-23). Milgrom suggests that "unclean" is used in relation to animals that make a person unclean either by consumption or through contact with their carcass, whereas "detestable" is used in relation to animals that are excluded from consumption but do not make a person unclean by touch (1991, 656-58).

Both "unclean" and "detestable" signify powerful negative states in the priestly traditions. The priestly reflection on God (its "theology") is significantly related to its system of purity and impurity. The latter provided one way by which the Israelites could locate themselves in relation to the holy. The system is grounded in the very good order of creation and provides a means of ordering the world. The priestly traditions think in terms of the practice of purity. The community must enact the world of purity and holiness.

The classification of the water creatures begins with the recognition of their location in the created order. The edible ones must reflect in their appearance, conduct, and locomotion their place within creation. Anomalies are excluded. Fins *and* scales are the identifying, one might say normative, characteristics of edible animals. The edible land animals and water creatures are both identified and "marked out" on the basis of bodily features.

Animals of the Air (vv. 13-19)

Verses 13-19 focus on the winged creatures of the air. An introductory statement indicates that the focus will be on the "detestable" *(sheqets)* birds (v. 13). The text provides a list of some twenty disqualified birds.

This unit does not specify the characteristics that identify edible birds; it simply names the excluded birds. Examination of the list suggests that the excluded birds are carrion birds (Milgrom 1991, 661-64; Houston 1993, 44-49). They eat the carcasses of dead animals or animals that they have killed. Thus, birds are identified by their location in creation, that is, animals of the air, but are excluded on the basis of their eating practices. Excluded birds are associated with blood consumption, an act strictly forbidden for the Israelite community (see Gen. 9:4-6; Lev. 3:17; 17:10-16), and with the pollution that arises from contact with a corpse in the field (cf. Lev. 11:39-40; Num. 19). The precise identification of every bird in the list is uncertain (see Levine 1989, 67-68; Milgrom 1991, 661-64; Hartley 1992, 159-60).

Winged Insects (vv. 20-23)

Verses 20-23 focus on winged insects. The structure of this unit is similar to the unit on land animals. An opening prohibitive statement (v. 20) is followed by a statement identifying the characteristics of edible insects (v. 21). A list of edible insects (v. 22) is followed by a concluding prohibition (v. 23). The anomaly of these creatures is readily apparent: winged insects that walk on all fours. The means of locomotion is not appropriate for their bodily appearance. They represent a disruption of the normative order as constructed by the priestly traditionists; they are "detestable" (vv. 20, 23).

There are, however, winged insects that may be eaten. They are identified by "jointed legs," which allow them to "leap" on the ground. Wings are consistent with leaping as a means of locomotion. Thus, they appropriately reflect their location within the created order. Four specific edible insects are identified: the locust, the bald locust, the cricket, and the grasshopper. In each case, the phrase "according to its kind" follows the naming of the insect. This is the language of creation found in Gen. 1 (see, e.g., vv. 11, 12, 24, 25), and it emphasizes the categories of creation that distinguish one type of creation from another. This separation and distinction is an effort to preserve and observe the good order of creation.

Contact with Carcasses (vv. 24-40)

Verses 24-40 discuss animals that make a person unclean through contact with their carcasses. In all probability, this unit is a later insertion into an existing text concerned with edible and inedible animals (vv. 1-23 and 41-43). Verses 24-40 may be divided into four basic parts: vv. 24-25; 26-28; 29-38; and 39-40. The instructions on purity are designed, in part, to maintain a careful distinction between situations associated with death and those associated with life. The boundary between life and death is dangerous and must be carefully guarded and maintained. Any possible contact with the realm of death must be ritually addressed.

Introduction (vv. 24-25)

The opening statement (vv. 24-25) provides a general framework. Detailed instructions will follow (vv. 26-40). The text distinguishes between "touching" and "carrying" in terms of the purification requirements (general instructions are found in vv. 24-25). The double purification requirement for "carrying" indicates that it was considered more severe because it constituted either more direct and intentional contact or more lengthy contact. The text provides a list of the specific animals and situations that can generate impurity.

Land Animals (vv. 26-28)

Verses 26-28 indicate that the carcasses of land animals prohibited as food (see vv. 2-8) make a person unclean through contact (v. 26). Any animal that walks on all four "paws" (as opposed to hoofs!) is unclean (v. 27). The purification rites reflect the distinction between touching and carrying (see vv. 24-25).

Swarming Creatures (vv. 29-38)

Verses 29-38 identify the swarming creatures that make a person unclean and related situations of impurity. The introductory statement is followed by a list of the swarming things that generate impurity through contact. The precise identification of these creatures is not certain. They were thought to have left their appropriate place in nature in order to "invade" or "violate" the human realm by entering into homes and areas of food storage (Carroll 1985, 120-24).

Contact with the carcasses of these animals makes one unclean until evening. A list of related situations of impurity is provided along with purification procedures (vv. 32-38). First, if their carcass falls on anything, whether an article of wood, cloth, skin, or sacking, that thing becomes unclean. The object must be dipped in water and becomes clean at evening (v. 32). Second, if the carcass falls into an earthen vessel, all that is in the vessel is unclean, and the vessel itself must be broken. Water from such a vessel contaminates any food or liquid with which it comes into contact (vv. 33-34). Third, objects on which the carcass falls — an oven and stove are specified — become unclean and must be broken (v. 35). The fear of passing along uncleanness through food and cooking seems particularly powerful.

There are some "exceptions" to the polluting power of animal carcasses (vv. 36-38). First, both a spring and a cistern remain clean, although anything within them becomes unclean if the carcass comes into contact with it. Seed that is dry, that is, seed that has not been watered or soaked in water, remains clean if the carcass touches it, whereas seed that has already been watered becomes unclean. The reason is clear: watered seeds are believed to have begun the growing process and are already on their way to becoming food.

Edible Animals (vv. 39-40)

Verses 39-40 provide instructions regarding the carcasses of edible animals that have died naturally. Anyone who touches the carcass is unclean until evening. A person who eats of the carcass or carries it must wash his or her clothing and wait until evening to become clean. Both the carcasses of inedible animals and the carcasses of edible animals communicate uncleanness through contact.

Swarming Creatures (vv. 41-45)

Verses 41-45 continue the dietary instructions of verses 2-23. They focus on swarming creatures (cf. vv. 29-38). An initial statement identifies swarming creatures as detestable *(shaqats)* and prohibits their consumption (v. 41). A detailed identification of swarming creatures follows (v. 42). Three characteristics are specified: whatever moves on its belly, whatever walks on all fours, and any creature that has many legs. The concluding statement (vv. 43-45) provides a theological basis for observing the instructions. These verses reflect both the style and spirit of the holiness code (Lev. 17-26; see Milgrom 1991, 691-97; Knohl 1995, 69).

The first prohibition (vv. 43-44) calls for the people to avoid making themselves detestable, defiled, and unclean. The reason is given in terms of a divine self-identification formula: I am Yahweh your God. The people are to avoid defilement because Yahweh is the God of Israel. A call to holiness follows. The prohibition against defilement leads to the identification of Yahweh as the one who brought them out of Egypt. Divine acts of redemption provide motivation for observing the prohibition. Something of

God's holiness may be seen and understood in and through God's actions in history. Likewise, Israel's holiness may be understood through Israel's actions in maintaining purity and order. The call for holiness reflects God's presence, God's redemptive activity, and God's participation in the ritual life of Israel.

Conclusion (vv. 46-47)

The conclusion of the chapter provides a summary of the instructions given in the text. The order of animals in this summary is different from that in the text, and the summary does not include a reference to winged insects (vv. 20-23). It also makes no mention of the issue of contact with carcasses, the focus of vv. 24-40. This chapter thus reflects a complex development.

The collections of instructions were clearly open to addition, adaptation, and clarification. The formation of these texts reflects an ongoing process of growth and development within communities that valued the instructions contained in the texts (see Fishbane 1985, 231-77). The texts reflect the dynamics of these communities — theological, sociological, ideological, and even psychological. Textual construction plays an important role in the development of community identity. Textual construction and community formation were parallel and interrelated processes (Sanders 1987, 11-39).

IMPURITY AND CHILDBIRTH (12:1-8)

Leviticus 12 contains instructions regarding impurity related to childbirth. Instructions are provided for the birth of a male child (vv. 2b-4), the birth of a female child (v. 5), the necessary rituals for purification (vv. 6-7), and special instructions for the poor (v. 8). Several difficult questions are raised concerning the nature and status of women. First, why is the woman considered unclean for giving birth when in fact procreation is part of God's blessing (Gen. 1:28)? Second, why must the woman enact a purification ritual when she clearly has not sinned? Third, why is the time for a mother's purification twice as long for a female child as it is for a male child?

For the contemporary reader, these questions give voice to the strangeness and otherness encountered in this text. It must be read within the context of the priestly system of purity and impurity. In addition, it must be recognized that this text forms a primary expression of the priestly construction of female sexuality and, therefore, a male understanding of female experience (see Plaskow 1990, 170-91; Frymer-Kensky 1989, 89-102). It raises difficult social, cultural, intellectual, and gender questions for the contemporary reader. Biblical interpretation (and this ultimately includes the formulation of "biblical" theology) is a construction that emerges out of a confrontation (in this case, "dialogue" is not strong enough!) between the ancient text and the contemporary reader.

The introductory statement addresses only Moses, and he is commanded to convey these instructions to the whole community (a shift from "Moses and Aaron" in Lev. 11). The instructions in ch. 12 are directed at the women in the community. They are the ones who will give birth, keep track of the days of impurity, and present the purificatory sacrifices and offerings. These instructions are not, therefore, primarily priestly matters! Indeed, the role of the priest is limited to the presentation of the sacrifices (see vv. 6-8 and compare the more extensive role of the priests in determining the status of skin diseases in ch. 13). Thus, the priestly traditions recognize the reality of women in the tabernacle ritual (see Gruber 1987).

The Birth of a Son (vv. 2b-4)

The first case addresses the birth of a male child (vv. 2b-4). The mother is ritually unclean for seven days. This impurity is compared to the impurity associated with menstruation. The mother is *not* considered unclean because of sin; giving birth was not considered a sin in Israel. Indeed, Gen. 1:28 states that human fertility actualizes the blessing of God. The reference to "as the time of her menstruation" may refer to the establishment of the *time* of impurity — it is *seven days* just as it is at the time of menstruation. Or, it may be a means of indicating the *reason* for the impurity — it is like the impurity associated with the flow of menstrual blood. Verse 7 suggests the latter reason: the purification ritual is designed to cleanse her "from her flow of blood." It is the blood associated with birth that places the new mother in a state of impurity (see the discussion of the birth of a daughter for additional possibilities). Following the seven days, there is an additional thirty-three days of purification after the birth of a male. During this time, the woman is not to touch any holy thing or come into the sanctuary (v. 4). She then brings her sacrifices and offerings to the sanctuary (vv. 6-8).

It is crucial to have some understanding of why the act of giving birth generates impurity for the new mother. The key is found in the priestly concern regarding defining and guarding the boundary that separates the realm of life from the realm of death. In the act of giving birth, the mother bodily enters into an ambiguous state between life and death. She brings a new life into the world, but, at the same time, she loses some of her own life through the loss of blood. The woman manifests the loss of life in the act of bringing forth a new life. It is the woman's location in this ambiguous state that generates her uncleanness: she holds together in her own body the realm of life and the realm of death (see Levine 1989, 249-50).

In comparing this impurity with the impurity associated with menstrual blood, the text indicates that the woman can communicate her uncleanness to others through contact (see Lev. 15:19-24). It may be that after the initial seven-day period she moves into a reduced state of impurity that requires only that she not touch anything holy (primarily the food of well-being offerings) and that she not enter the sanctuary (Milgrom 1991, 749-50). Purification from the impurity associated with birth entails a *process* of purification, which marks the birth as a significant event and locates it in the context of the sacred.

Verse 3 provides instructions for the circumcision of a male child. It is to take place on the eighth day after his birth. This coincides with the end of the mother's seven days of impurity. The child is not unclean. Circumcision was the ritual by which a male became a part of the covenant community (see Gen. 17:9-14). It was a ritual enactment of the covenant and the promise of fertility. Significantly, there is no indication that the blood of circumcision makes the male baby unclean. Whereas the blood associated with birth makes the mother unclean and excludes her from the sacred, the blood associated with circumcision functions to include the male in the community! This "ritual" text juxtaposes the image of the woman giving birth, an image that connects her to the blessing of God given in creation, with the image of the circumcised male, an image that connects him to the blessing of God given in covenant. It is precisely in this juxtaposition that one can see the ambiguous nature of blood — it can function to exclude and to include (see Eilberg-Schwartz 1990, 141-94).

The Birth of a Daughter (v. 5)

The time of impurity for the new mother is twice as long if she gives birth to a daughter: fourteen days as opposed to seven for the initial period with the birth of a son, and sixty-six days as opposed to thirty-three for the period of purification (v. 5). This suggests that the flow of blood associated with birth is only part of the reason for the mother's impurity and supports the earlier contention that the unclean state is related to the ambiguous situation generated by the act of giving birth. It has been suggested that the birth of a female child was considered less valuable and, therefore, required a longer period of purification (this is usually based on the relative value of males and females established in Lev. 27:2-7, which, however, focuses on "labor" value more than "inherent" value). The reasoning of such a view is not clear. Why would the *less* valued bring *greater* impurity (see Gruber 1987, 43 n. 13)? The birth of a female created another woman capable of giving birth. The key is that the female child has the potential to share in the experience of giving birth (Levine 1989, 249-50). This text thus places great significance on the ability of women to give birth. It does not argue that this is the primary role of women, and it does not devalue women in their role as mothers. It does, however, attempt to "hedge about," ritualize, and control the process of giving birth. As such, it reflects an effort to control female sexuality.

After the appropriate time of purification passes, the mother must enact the purification ritual (v. 6-8). She must bring a burnt offering and a purification offering. The purification offering would be presented first (see Levine 1965). In this instance, the burnt offering expresses the mother's gratitude for the birth of the child. "Expiation" (v. 8) refers to the ritual process that effects the movement of the woman from a state of impurity to a state of purity. It has to do with passage and relocation.

Verse 8 allows a woman to bring two turtledoves or two pigeons for her offering — one for a burnt offering and one for a purification offering. The economic concession for the poor is necessary in that this is a required ritual.

UNCLEAN SKIN DISEASES AND GROWTHS (CHS. 13–14)

Leviticus 13–14 seek to identify unclean skin diseases that appear on persons, clothing, or the walls of houses and provide purification rituals to be enacted when the impurity disappears. The primary concern is to identify growths that are *tsara'at,* traditionally translated "leprosy." *Tsara'at* is not leprosy as defined by medical science. It refers to a wide range of skin diseases, irritations, eruptions, and fungal growths and may, in certain respects, reflect a schematic idealization of unclean skin diseases and growths (see Wright and Jones 1992).

These chapters provide (1) instructions for the priestly determination and declaration of the status of a person or object in regard to purity (13:2-44 [persons], 47-58 [clothing]; 14:34-53 [houses]), (2) instructions for the actions to be taken if a person or object is declared unclean because of *tsara'at* (13:45-46 [persons], 47-58 [clothing; identification and resultant action are discussed together]; 14:34-53 [houses; identification and resultant action are discussed together]), and (3) instructions for the ritual of purification, which takes place if and when a person recovers from *tsara'at* (14:2-32).

These chapters do not have a medical concern. The priest is not a doctor and the afflicted person is not a patient. The concern is the identification of unclean skin eruptions or fungal growths. These instructions reflect the priestly system of purity and impurity and the concern to maintain the purity and holiness of the divine dwelling. The priest is a cultic specialist who examines skin diseases and determines whether they are clean or unclean. In this way, the priest "separates" the clean and the unclean (see 10:10).

Two primary reasons explain the priestly concern for skin eruptions. First, they were thought to be one means by which God punished "sinful" people. For example, Miriam breaks out with *tsara'at* because she challenged the status of Moses as the rightful mediator of the word of Yahweh (Num. 12). Elisha "curses" Gehazi with *tsara'at* because the latter was deceitful and greedy (2 Kings 5:27). Yahweh strikes King Uzziah with *tsara'at* when the king offered incense in the temple against the orders of the priests (2 Chron. 26:16-21; cf. Deut. 24:8). Thus, *tsara'at* may be an indication of sin and divine punishment. Second, *tsara'at* is associated with diseases that eat away at the body. The case of Miriam is instructive. Aaron asks that she not be "like one born dead, who, when coming out of its mother's womb, has half of its flesh eaten away" (Num. 12:12). Such skin diseases were associated with the realm of decay and death. The comparison of *tsara'at* with snow is telling. The emphasis is clearly on the *snowflake* and not on the whiteness of the snow (see Exod. 4:6; Num. 12:10; 2 Kings 5:27, "white" is not in the Hebrew). One of the telling factors in the impurity associated with these diseases is that they appear to result in the "flaking" away of the skin (Wright and Jones 1992, 277-78). The skin is being eaten away as if it is dead. The realm of the holy had to be carefully guarded and protected from this living death.

Although it is not possible at the present time to identify precisely the seven types of unclean "diseases," it is clear that they reflect a concern for the integrity of the body. The encroachment of death is seen in flaking, decaying, or rotting flesh. The priestly traditions seek to protect the integrity and wholeness of the body, which reflects the wholeness and integrity both of the holy and of society (see Pilch 1981).

Determining Clean and Unclean Skin Problems (13:1-44)

These instructions were spoken to both Moses and Aaron (v. 1). The priests must understand these instructions because they must identify the impurities. Verses 2-44 outline seven possible situations or cases and indicate how they are to be addressed by the priest (vv. 2-8; 9-17; 18-23; 24-28; 29-37; 38-39; 40-44).

Case One (vv. 2-8)

When a person has a skin swelling, eruption, irritation, or dis- coloration, the matter is brought to the attention of the priest for examination and declaration. If the hair in the diseased area has turned white and the area appears deeper than the skin, the person is pronounced unclean (v. 3). If, however, the spot is no deeper than the skin and the hair has not turned white, then a twenty-one day process begins (vv. 4-8). If the disease has not spread during that time, the person is declared clean. If it spreads, then the person is unclean. A disease that appears "deeper than the skin" is viewed as "eating" into the skin and is declared unclean.

Case Two (vv. 9-17)

When a person shows signs of a scaly skin disease, the priest examines the person. If there is a white swelling in the skin, the hair is white, and there is evidence of raw flesh, the person is declared unclean (vv. 10-11). If the disease has covered the whole body and turned white, it is clean (vv. 12-13). If the flesh is raw, the person is unclean. If, however, at a later time it turns white, the person is reexamined and declared clean (vv. 14-16). In this case, it is the appearance of "raw flesh" that is determinative. This suggests a "decaying" of the skin.

Case Three (vv. 18-23)

The third case deals with boils that have healed. If either a white swelling appears or a reddish-white spot, the priest must make an examination. If the spot is deeper than the skin and the hair is white, it is unclean (v. 20). If it is neither white nor deeper than the skin, reexamination takes place in seven days. If the disease spreads, the person is unclean. If not, the person is clean (vv. 21-23). The characteristics of "unclean" are similar to those in the first case.

Case Four (vv. 24-28)

If a person has a burn and the burn becomes a spot that is either reddish or white, the priest must make an examination. If the hair is white and the spot is deeper than the skin, the person is unclean (v. 25). If the hair is not white and the spot is not deeper than the skin, the person is reexamined in seven days. If the disease spreads, the person is unclean. If not, the person is clean (vv. 26-28).

Case Five (vv. 29-37)

This case addresses a skin disease in the hair or beard. If the spot appears to be deeper than the skin and the hair has turned yellow and thin, the person is pronounced unclean (v. 30). If the spot is not deeper than the skin and has no black hair in it, the person is confined for seven days. At that time, if the itch has not spread, there is no yellow hair, and the spot is not deeper than the skin, the person shaves (the hair, but not the itch). Following another seven days, if the disease has not spread, the person is declared clean and must wash her or his clothes (vv. 31-34). If the itch spreads at a later time or if it "recovers," the initial declaration may be reversed (vv. 35-37).

Case Six (vv. 38-39)

This passage describes an outbreak of dull, white spots on the body. If they do not show the signs of the decay and eating away found in unclean eruptions, then the person is declared clean.

Case Seven (vv. 40-44)

This unit states that baldness, either from the head or the forehead and temples, is not unclean. If, however, there is a reddish-white spot, the priest makes an examination. If the eruption resembles a *tsara'at* disease, the person is pronounced unclean.

Unclean Individuals (13:45-46)

This unit prescribes behavior for a person declared unclean because of *tsara'at*. The instructions contain three basic elements. First, these persons must wear torn clothes, dishevel their hair, cover their upper lip, and cry out, "Unclean, unclean!" This is a public enactment of the disease. The "decay" of the body is reflected in the "decay" of the social appearance. Others are warned to keep a safe distance. Second, the person remains unclean as long as the disease is present. The disease makes the person unclean; the priestly pronouncement makes the unclean state a social and ritual reality. Third, the person is excluded from the social body lest the social body become unclean through its embodiment of the realm of death (cf. Num 5:1-3). In addition, the dwelling of Yahweh must be protected from impurity. Ritual expulsion is one means by which the priestly traditionists constructed, defined, watched over, and attempted to control the social body.

Unclean Clothing (13:47-59)

This unit focuses on clothing — woolen, linen, or hide — that displays *tsara'at,* identified as a greenish or reddish spot. In this case, the "disease" is best understood as mold or fungal growths. The garment is taken to the priest for examination, who sets it aside for seven days and then reexamines it. If the disease has spread, it is identified as *tsara'at* and the garment is burned (vv. 51-52). If the disease has not spread, the garment is washed and put aside for seven more days. If, at that time, the spot has not changed color, the garment is unclean and must be burned (vv. 53-55). If the diseased area has begun to fade after it was washed, the priest tears out the spot. If, however, it appears again, the disease is spreading and the garment must be burned (vv. 56-57). If the spot disappears after the garment is washed, then it is washed a second time and is clean (v. 58). The focus is on whether the material has the appearance of rot, decay, or disintegration. Verse 59 closes the instruction *(torah)* concerning diseased spots in clothing material.

Purification Rituals (14:1-57)

Leviticus 14 contains three primary units: the purification ritual for a person who has "recovered" from a *tsara'at* disease (vv. 2-32); instructions for identifying *tsara'at* in a house and the purification ritual for an unclean house (vv. 34-53); and a summary statement that serves as a conclusion to chapters 13-14 (vv. 54-57). There are two introductory statements (vv. 1, 33).

Rituals for the Recovered Individual (14:2-32)

The ritual process for the person who has recovered from an unclean skin disease is complex and reflects elements of older practices. The person with *tsara'at* who is pronounced unclean must live alone and dwell outside the camp (13:46). The purification ritual is designed, in part, to move a person back into society (see Gorman 1990, 161-79). The rules regarding purity and associated ritual processes function to locate persons within existing societal structures, to remove and exclude them when they pose a danger, and to restore them when they no longer pose a threat.

The person declared unclean because of a skin disease is placed outside the camp. That person, through expulsion, experiences social death. Ritual expulsion, then, functions not only to protect society from impurity but also to enact and embody the "contact with death" associated with *tsara'at* in "lived" experience. The "death" associated with *tsara'at* is made a social reality through the expulsion from the community. The ritual process, then, must restore the person to a place within society. The complete ritual process covers eight days, and specific ritual actions take place in three distinct locations on three specific days. The ritual brings about passage, movement, and relocation.

Day One (vv. 2-8): The ritual activity of this day is designed to move the person from outside the camp to inside the camp. The expulsion is a form of social death, reflecting the "death" of the skin disease; the ritual functions to restore the person to life and the community. This ritual is not a healing ritual but a ritual designed to move a person already recovered back into a place within the community.

When the person recovers, the priest goes outside the camp to make an examination. If the person is declared clean, the ritual process begins. The materials used include two living clean birds, cedarwood, crimson yarn, and hyssop (cf. the purification ritual for corpse contamination in Num. 19:6). Two primary activities take place. First, one of the birds is slaughtered over fresh, running (Heb. "living") water (cf. Lev. 15:13), and the living bird is dipped in the blood and released. Second, the person shaves, launders his or her clothes, and bathes.

The "living" water images the overall function of the ritual — to move the individual into life. In the same way, the use of the two birds provides a graphic image of the larger purpose of the ritual. The blood of the slaughtered bird juxtaposes the symbolic values of death and life — it is slaughtered in order to provide blood with the life in it (see Gen. 9:4-5; Lev. 17:11). The manipulation of the blood collapses these normally distinct categories in order to reconstruct them and, thereby, reestablish the boundary between them. The death of one bird reflects the "death" of the person expulsed because of an impure skin disease. The living bird is dipped into the blood and is released. In this way, the "death" associated with the skin impurity is removed (cf. the "removal" of the sins of the nation on the head of the "live" goat in Lev. 16:20-22). The "death" of the individual is concretized and actualized in the slaughtered bird, whereas the "life" toward which the recovered individual is ritually moving is concretized and actualized in the living bird.

The final actions — shaving, laundering, bathing — of the first day embody the state into which the individual has now moved. The new state is declared by the priest. The changed ritual status, generated by the ritual and declared by the priest, is now "bodied" forth. The person enters the camp but remains outside her or his tent. Initial entry into the camp is necessary in order for the sacrifices and offerings to be presented at the entrance of the tent.

Day Seven (v. 9): This is a transitional day. The shaving, laundering, and bathing effect cleansing and prepare the individual for the remainder of the ritual. They "mark out" the person and anticipate the new status that is being constructed in, by, and through the larger ritual process.

Day Eight (vv. 10-20): On the eighth day, the person brings two male lambs and one ewe lamb, a grain offering, and a measure of oil to the priest at the entrance of the tent. One lamb is raised as an elevation offering and will be presented as a reparation offering (see 7:28-36). The blood of this lamb will be placed on the right earlobe, the right thumb, and the right big toe of the individual.

The reparation offering is required because skin diseases were viewed, at times, as a form of divine punishment for trespass or improper use of holy things (see the "Introduction" to chs. 13–14). This offering addresses the possibility of trespass against sancta (see 5:14–6:7 [Heb. 5:14-26]). The placing of the blood on the extremities is a crucial aspect of this ritual. The ordination of the priesthood provides the only parallel, although in that case the blood of the ram of ordination is used (see 8:22-24). Both of these ritual processes function to move persons from one state to another, and, in both cases, the passage is across dangerous lines that separate one category from another. The blood on the *extremities* effects the passage of the "whole" individual from one state to another.

The oil used in the elevation offering is sprinkled seven times before Yahweh. Some of it is placed on the extremities of the person and on top of the blood of the reparation offering, and the rest is poured on the individual's head. The oil reflects the "life" the person has now ritually experienced and indicates that the passage from "outside" to "inside" has been accomplished.

The presentation of a purification offering and a burnt offering does not necessarily indicate that the person has sinned. Impurity was generated that polluted the sacred tent. The purification offering functions to cleanse the tent of this impurity. The burnt offering, in this case, ritually enacts the joy and celebration experienced by the individual. In this way, the priest enacts expiation *(kipper)* for the person, and the person is cleansed (v. 20b). "Expiation" here refers to the restoration of the person to life within the community.

Verses 21-32 present parallel instructions for those who cannot afford the more expensive materials. These persons are to bring a male lamb for a reparation offering, one-tenth of an ephah of fine flour along with oil, and two turtledoves or pigeons for the purification and burnt offerings. The ritual follows the pattern indicated above.

Rituals for a "Diseased" House (14:33-53)

Verses 33-53 focus on identifying and addressing diseased growths on the walls of houses and has its own introductory formula: "Yahweh spoke to Moses and Aaron" (v. 33). The instructions concern fungal growths and are intended for the people when they enter the land of Canaan (v. 34). Instructions for "diseased" *houses* would not be of great concern for people living in tents in the wilderness! Interestingly, Yahweh takes responsibility for putting such a "disease" on houses (v. 34).

If a growth or disease is found, the owner must report the matter to the priest, who goes and examines the house. Before the examination, everything is brought out of the house lest it is declared unclean and is lost. The communication of impurity by the house to other objects can only take place after the priest makes a pronouncement.

If greenish or reddish spots appear that are deeper than the wall, the house is shut up for seven days. If the examination on the seventh day reveals that the spots have spread, all the diseased material is thrown into an unclean place outside the city. The unclean material is removed from the city in order to protect the city from contamination (cf. the "clean" place outside the city in 4:12; 6:11 [Heb. 6:4]). The wall is repaired. If the house becomes diseased again, it is torn down and thrown into an unclean place outside the city. The house can contaminate those who enter it (until evening), sleep in it (wash their clothes and wait until evening), or eat in it (wash clothes and wait until evening).

If, however, the "disease" has not spread on the seventh day, it is pronounced clean; the disease is "healed" (v. 48). The house must be ritually purified (vv. 49-53). The basic structure of the ritual is similar to the ritual for the recovered leper. The house is sprinkled with the blood of a bird and water, which "cleanses" the house (v. 52). In addition, the release is crucial to the priestly enactment of expiation (*kipper;* v. 53). Clearly, the house did not sin, and thus the expiation does not refer to sin. It refers to cleansing and restoration.

Conclusion (14:54-57)

The concluding verses indicate that the instructions for identifying and addressing unclean growths are now concluded. The instructions were provided in order to distinguish between the clean and the unclean and to guide the priesthood in making such determinations.

BODILY DISCHARGES (CH. 15)

Leviticus 15 addresses impurity arising from bodily discharges. The text focuses on various types of "flow" *(zab)* from the body, with particular emphasis on discharges associated with the reproductive organs. These instructions reflect a concern for the integrity of the boundaries of the body. The focus on the reproductive organs reflects a desire to locate the creation of life within the larger system of ritual and purity. It is one means by which the divine promise and blessing are connected to the ritual system.

The text discusses common and everyday situations that *might* arise and identifies impurity in relation to bodily discharges. It seeks to locate sexual activity within the larger context of religion and ritual. The instructions indicate that such discharges must be ritually "watched over" and "contextualized." The bodily discharges ultimately reflect the priestly struggle to separate the realm of life from the realm of death (Wenham 1983).

The instructions are theologically related to the blessing of God in creation, the blessing that human beings be fruitful and multiply (Gen. 1:28). A ritual "watch" is placed on the blessing. In addition, these instructions are related to the divine promise of many descendants (e.g., Gen. 17:4-7). The chapter locates both the body and sexuality within the context of theological reflection and ritual.

Yahweh speaks to both Moses and Aaron, although the instructions are intended for the whole community (vv. 1-2a). The chapter details the types of discharges that make one unclean, the ways in which others can become unclean through various kinds of contact, and instructions for enacting the necessary rituals of purification for those who have become unclean because of discharges.

The chiastic structure of the chapter is significant (see Whitekettle 1991, 34-37; Hartley 1992, 205-7). An introductory statement (vv. 1-2a) is matched by a concluding statement (vv. 31-33). Instructions on abnormal discharges in males (vv. 2b-15) and normal male discharges (vv. 16-17) are matched by instructions on normal female discharges (vv. 19-24) and abnormal discharges in females (vv. 25-30). At the center of the text are instructions concerning sexual intercourse (v. 18).

Abnormal Discharges: Male (vv. 2b-15)

A man who has a discharge from his sexual organ is unclean (v. 2b). This refers to a "flow" unrelated to sexual activity (it is not semen) or to fluid that prohibits normal activities (v. 3). Either of these abnormal situations makes the man unclean.

Such impurity can be communicated to other persons and objects. Two general statements provide the framework for the discussion of how such impurity is communicated. First, every bed on which the unclean person lies and every object on which he sits are unclean (v. 4). Second, every riding seat on which he sits is unclean (v. 9). The text specifies ten situations in which a man's uncleanness is communicated to other persons (vv. 5-12). There are four basic types of rulings in these verses. First, general statements are given concerning a bed, a seat, or a saddle (vv. 4, 9). Anyone who touches the bed or sits on the seat of an unclean person becomes unclean (vv. 5-6). Anyone who touches anything that was under the unclean man becomes unclean, and all who carry such a thing are unclean (v. 10). These statements refer to the practical concerns that arise in removing a riding seat from an animal. Second, impurity is communicated if the unclean person either spits on another (v. 8) or touches another with unrinsed hands (v. 11). Third, a person becomes unclean if he or she touches the unclean person (v. 7). Fourth, both an earthen vessel and a wooden vessel become unclean through contact (v. 12).

There are three distinct purification processes detailed in the text. Persons who become unclean through contact must (1) wash the clothes that they were wearing at the time the impurity was contracted; (2) bathe their entire body in water; and (3) wait until evening to be clean. In one instance, the person is only required to wait until evening to be clean (v. 10, although the other two activities may be assumed, see Milgrom 1991, 919). Leviticus 11:24-28 makes a similar distinction between touching and carrying an unclean object (a carcass). A third ruling indicates that an earthen vessel touched by the unclean person must be broken; a wooden vessel may be cleansed simply by rinsing it. Earthen vessels were thought to be more susceptible to uncleanness than wooden ones (cf. 11:32-33).

Verses 13-15 prescribe the purification process for a man who has recovered from his discharge. Seven days after the discharge stops, he must launder his clothes and bathe his body in fresh ("living") water. A seven-day period marks the necessary time for the ritual passage from one state to another, especially in those situations in which the passage is across dangerous boundaries (e.g., 8:33; 14:8-9). The water used in the laundering and bathing restores the person to a state of purity ("living" water is also specified in Num. 19:17 and Lev. 14:5-6).

On the eighth day, sacrifices and offerings are presented. Either two turtledoves or two pigeons must be brought, one for a purification offering and one for a burnt offering. The priest offers them to enact expiation *(kipper)* on behalf of the person. The impurity associated with genital discharge is attracted to the sanctuary and defiles sacred space. The purification offering cleanses the sanctuary; the burnt offering enacts the person's gratitude for the reality of purification and restoration.

Normal Discharges: Male (vv. 16-17)

These two verses address the impurity associated with an emission of semen (cf. Deut. 23:10-11 [Heb. vv. 11-12]). This is a "normal" emission, although not one associated with sexual intercourse (that is addressed in v. 18). The man must bathe his body in water and wait until evening to be clean. Any material or skin on which the semen falls is unclean. It must be washed and will be clean in the evening.

Sexual Intercourse (v. 18)

If a man and a woman have sexual intercourse and the man has an emission of semen, both people become unclean. This situation is viewed as a relatively minor form of impurity, and cleansing requires only bathing and waiting until evening. In light of the divine blessing of creation (Gen. 1:28), this form of impurity is unexpected.

These instructions reflect the priestly desire to keep watch over both the boundaries of the body and reproductive activity.

Sexual intercourse, in which the male has an emission of semen, may generate life. The possible creation of life brings the persons into proximity with the realm of death. The boundaries of the body have been disrupted. An ambiguous situation is created: life and death are brought together; impurity is generated. The text says nothing about the ethics of sexual activity, nor does it suggest that sexual intercourse is sinful. It is concerned with impurity.

Normal Discharges: Female (vv. 19-24)

A woman's regular discharge of blood in menstruation makes her unclean "for seven days." It is not certain if this refers to the actual days of blood loss or to seven days beyond the conclusion of her flow. However, these traditions normally indicate if an additional seven days is required for purification, so it is probable that the time of impurity is limited to the days of menstruation. During this time, a woman can communicate her impurity to others through contact. Cleansing requires laundering clothes, bathing, and the arrival of evening (vv. 21-23). Contact with a bed on which the woman lies or a seat on which she sits makes a person unclean (v. 20; cf. vv. 5-12). In addition, if a man lies with her and some of her "impurity" falls on him, he is unclean for seven days and can communicate uncleanness to any bed on which he lies during this period (v. 24).

The impurity associated with menstruation creates a rhythm of regular exclusion and uncleanness for the woman. For many contemporary readers this is a harsh and sexist ruling. This is particularly true in that the text makes semen and menstrual blood parallel (cf. vv. 16-17 and vv. 19-24). Thus, many view this as an effort on the part of an exclusively male priesthood to exercise control over women's bodies by declaring that menstrual blood is unclean and, on that basis, regulating women's activity (see Plaskow 1990, 171-210). There are, for better or worse, however, theological and conceptual issues at work in these instructions that link them to the larger priestly system of purity and impurity. Three key concerns are operative. First, the flow of blood disrupts the integrity of the boundaries of the body, which the priestly traditionists sought to watch over (they watched over male as well as female bodies). Second, and very closely related to the first, is the concern associated with the passage of blood from the reproductive organs of the body. The priests sought to "interpret" genital discharges through rulings on impurity. Third, the rulings reflect the priestly understanding of blood — life is in it. The flow of blood is viewed as a loss of life. The woman is located at the intersection of life and death, an ambiguous situation (on the blood of circumcision, see 12:2b-4).

Abnormal Discharges: Female (vv. 25-30)

These verses discuss "abnormal" flows of blood: a flow at a time distinct from menstruation or a flow that extends beyond "normal" menstruation. The woman is unclean for the entire time of the discharge in the same way that she is unclean during her menstrual flow (v. 25). Both beds and seats may become unclean and communicate uncleanness to others through contact (vv. 26-27). The ritual for her purification is the same as that for a man with a genital discharge (vv. 28-30; see the discussion of vv. 13-15).

Concluding Statement (vv. 31-33)

Verses 31-33 contain two concluding notes. The first functions as a conclusion to chapters 11–15 (v. 31; cf. 10:10). It makes clear that ritual uncleanness can defile the tabernacle even when such impurity is not the result of sin. Impurity threatens the integrity of sacred space and violates the divine dwelling place. The second functions as a conclusion to the instructions on unclean discharges (vv. 32-33).

THE DAY OF PURIFICATION (CH. 16)

Leviticus 16 prescribes the ritual for the annual day of purification, in which the sacred area is cleansed and the sins of the people are removed from the camp. The chapter serves as a conclusion to the chapters dealing with impurity (11–15). This ritual functions to cleanse the sacred area of those impurities left unaddressed during the year. At the same time, it refers back to the death of Aaron's two sons (see ch. 10), when "they drew near before Yahweh" (v. 1). The chapter addresses, in part, the problem created by the presence of their corpses in the holy area (Kiuchi 1987, 67-85; Milgrom 1991, 635-40). The instructions are significantly related both to the narrative of the founding of the tabernacle and to the instructions on purity and impurity. Ritual concerns and narrative concerns are interwoven in a text that might best be described as "narrative prescription."

The chapter addresses two distinct, but interrelated questions: (1) How is it possible to draw near to Yahweh without dying in the process? (2) How is it possible to maintain the purity of the sacred area in the context of community impurities and the death of Aaron's two sons? This text prescribes the ritual process that allows Aaron to enter safely into the holy place and to enact the prescribed ritual of purification in the heart of the holy place. However, the possibility of death remains ("lest he die!"); entrance is fraught with danger!

In this ritual, and only in this ritual, blood is brought behind the veil into the holy of holies. On this day, the high priest enters the most holy place and places blood on and before the ark. The juxtaposition of these cultic realities — the divine presence in the holy of holies and the impurities of the community — and Aaron's ritual entry into the midst of this ambiguous and "impossible" situation creates both narrative and ritual tension.

This is a community ritual that takes place once a year. It is both a rite of passage and a rite of restoration. It moves the community from a state of impurity to a state of purity (passage) and restores the integrity of the holy place, the community, and the very good order of creation. The contexts within which human existence takes shape — creation, cult, and society — have been disrupted, and this ritual restores them to their more normal status. The dynamics of this ritual reflect the priestly concern for the movement between chaos and order (cf. Gen. 1:1–2:4a in which creation is imaged as a movement from chaos to order). This ritual enacts order.

The Ritual Proper

The ritual process begins with the gathering of the necessary materials (vv. 3, 5). At the heart of the ritual is Aaron's entry into the holy of holies. This part of the ritual is "marked off" by parallel acts of washing and enclothement (vv. 4, 23-24). While Aaron is in this ritually "marked off" state, he fills the holy of holies with smoke, sprinkles blood on the ark and the altar of burnt offerings, and places the sins of the community, through confession, on the head of a goat that will be released (for Azazel) in the wilderness. After the second washing and clothing rite, Aaron offers the burnt offerings.

The Clothing of Aaron (v. 4)
Aaron washes his body and puts on linen undergarments, a linen tunic with sash, and a linen turban. The "holy" vestments on this day are distinct from the magnificent garments prescribed for the high priest in Exod. 28 (cf. Exod. 39:1-31). The linen clothes are "common." This is a day of national humiliation (see vv. 29-34), and the priest functions as the representative of the people. The common linen clothing reflects his common (representative) status. The ritual enclothement marks his status as the representative of the people and identifies him with the people. The washing cleanses him and prepares him for further ritual activity.

The Presentation of the Two Live Goats (vv. 7-10)
Two goats are brought to the entrance of the tent and lots are cast over them. One goat is designated for Yahweh; the other is designated for Azazel. The goat selected for Yahweh will serve as the purification offering for the people, whereas the goat selected for Azazel will be sent, carrying the sins of the people, into the wilderness (see the discussion below).

The Smoking Censer (vv. 12-13)
Aaron takes a censer filled with coals from the altar and incense and fills the holy of holies with smoke. He does this to cover the seat of expiation (*hakkapporet*) lest he die (vv. 12-13). Yahweh

dwells inside the holy of holies above the ark of the covenant, and entry into this area is dangerous. The smoke acts, in part, to protect Aaron from direct encounter with the divine presence. At the same time — and the juxtaposition is of importance — the smoke functions as an indication that Yahweh is indeed present in the holy of holies. In all probability, this smoke is associated with the smoke on top of Sinai. The priestly traditionists emphasize that the glory of Yahweh took up residence in the holy of holies (cf. Exod. 24:15-18 and Exod. 40:34-38). The smoke in the holy of holies functions to "veil" and at the same time to "reveal" the presence of Yahweh (Gorman 1990, 70-71; Mann 1971).

The Purification Offerings (vv. 11, 14, 15-19)

The purification offerings are central in this ritual. After filling the room with smoke, Aaron slaughters the bull for himself, takes some of its blood into the holy of holies, and sprinkles the blood with his finger seven times "on the front of" and "before" the seat of expiation. Two separate actions are indicated. The blood "on the front" purifies *and* the blood "before" reconsecrates (see Lev. 4). The sevenfold sprinkling indicates the more serious nature of this particular use of the blood — the blood is brought into the holy of holies only once a year. "The seat of expiation" is traditionally rendered as "the mercy seat" *(hakkapporet,* related to *kipper)* and refers to the lid placed on top of the ark of the covenant. It is above this "seat" that the divine presence is said to dwell. The word might be rendered "the heart of expiation" or "the place where community expiation is enacted." This is a place that has to do with expiation and divine presence.

Although normally people slaughter their own sacrificial animals, that is not practical here — every member of the community cannot be involved in the actual ritual. Thus, Aaron, as the representative of the people, slaughters the goat for the people. He takes the blood of the goat inside the holy of holies and sprinkles its blood in the same way that he sprinkled the blood of the bull. In this way, he enacts "expiation" *(kipper)*. Verse 16 explains that the blood of the purification sacrifices cleanses the tent from the impurities of the community.

While Aaron is inside the holy of holies, no one else is to enter the tent (v. 17). This reflects the danger associated with his entry into the most holy place. It also suggests that Aaron's entry into the holy of holies is the central activity in this ritual.

Aaron exits the tent, places some of the blood of both the bull and the goat on the four horns of the altar, and sprinkles some of it seven times on the altar. In this way he cleanses *and* reconsecrates the altar (v. 19). The twofold manipulation of the blood reflects not only the need to purify sacred objects, but also the need to reconstitute the integrity of the holy. Impurity defiles and disrupts; ritual cleanses and restores.

The Goat for Azazel (vv. 20-22)

Aaron presents the live goat that is to be sent to Azazel. He places both of his hands on the head of the goat and confesses over it all the iniquities, transgressions, and sins of the people of Israel. As representative of the people, Aaron confesses their sins and places them on the head of the goat.

This is a rite of banishment (cf. the living bird in 14:7). Several issues, however, must be clarified in order to understand what "banishment" means in this ritual. First, Aaron places both of his hands on the head of the goat and confesses the sins of the community (see 1:3-4). Aaron's voice functions as the voice of the people. In this ritual act of confession, the priest creates the sins in order that he may take them in hand and place them on the goat. This is not "simply" a symbolic act. The sins are ritually placed on the goat so that it may carry them into the wilderness (certainly not a symbolic carrying, which, if taken to extremes, might eventuate in a symbolic goat!). The high priest actualizes or concretizes the sins through confession and puts them on the goat, which carries them into the wilderness, away from the camp.

Second, the text states that the living goat is for Azazel. Various explanations of "Azazel" exist (for a review, see Hartley 1992, 237-38), but Azazel is best viewed as a wilderness being, not unlike a demonic being, who is associated with the powers of chaos (see Tawil 1980, 47-59). Third, Israel's traditions often associate chaos and danger with the wilderness (e.g., Num. 20:4-5; Isa. 34:9-16; Jer. 4:23-26). The wilderness is viewed as chaotic, in part, because it occupies an ambiguous position in Israel's story. The structure of the larger narrative reflects the dynamics of a rite of passage (see Cohn 1981, 7-23; Thompson 1981, 355-58): Passover in Egypt (Exod. 12), passage through the Red Sea (Exod. 14–15), journey in the wilderness (Exod. 16–18), the Sinai covenant and instructions (Exod. 19:1–Num. 10:10), journey in the wilderness (Num. 10:11–Deut. 34:12), passage through the Jordan River (Josh. 3–4), and Passover in the land of Canaan (Josh. 5:10-12). The "wilderness" is located "betwixt and between" Israel's life of slavery in Egypt and its life of freedom in Canaan. The wilderness is a liminal state, a time and place in which normal structures do not hold. Israel is in the process of moving from one status to another, in transition. Liminal states are ambiguous because the normal structures of everyday life are not operative, and liminal states are often depicted as chaotic. Thus, the wilderness, the place in which Israel was already free but not yet home, came to be viewed as a place of chaos, ambiguous and dangerous (Gorman 1990, 95-100).

Azazel dwells in the wilderness and embodies the chaos associated with it. The goat bears the sins of the people into this place of chaos. The intention is clear: the sins of the people create impurity that pollutes the tabernacle, and Yahweh cannot dwell in the midst of impurity. The departure of the divine presence would result in chaos for the nation precisely because Yahweh's presence in their midst is central to and constitutive of Israel's self-identity in the priestly traditions. Thus, sins, the cause of pollution and possible chaos, are put in their place; they are sent to Azazel and placed in the realm of chaos. In this way they are removed from the camp.

The Final Washing and Clothing of Aaron (vv. 23-24a)

Following the sending of the goat into the wilderness, Aaron again washes and changes his clothing. An examination of Aaron's role up to this point will clarify the dynamics of the ritual. This is a rite of passage that moves the community from impurity (chaos) to purity (order). As such, it is a liminal day. Aaron embodies this larger structure (see Gorman 1990, 90-95). He washes and changes his clothes in order to mark his entry into and exit out of a liminal state. While in this liminal state, he embodies the "impossible." He is holy because he was anointed with the holy anointing oil (Lev. 8:12). At the same time, he becomes impure when he confesses the sins of the people and *places* those sins on the head of the goat. He holds together in himself holiness *and* impurity. Ritual makes the "impossible" possible. The ritual collapses normal structures (i.e., keeping the holy separated from the impure) in order to reconstruct them. The high priest enacts and actualizes this deconstruction and reconstruction.

The Burnt Offerings and Other Instructions (vv. 24b-28)

Aaron offers the burnt offerings for himself and for the people and burns the fat of the purification offerings (v. 25). The one who frees the goat in the wilderness must undertake a minor purification ritual (v. 26). The goat for Azazel was impure and capable of defiling others. The remains of the bull and the goat are taken outside the camp and burned (v. 27 and cf. 6:23). The one who burns them must undertake a minor purification ritual before reentering the camp.

Concluding Summary (vv. 29-34)

Although the concluding summary statement is, in all likelihood, a later addition to the text, it constitutes an important interpretive statement concerning the annual ritual (cf. Lev. 23:26-32; Num. 29:7-11). It states that the ritual is to take place on the tenth day of the seventh month (v. 29; cf. Lev. 23:26 and Num. 29:7). On this day, the people are to "deny" themselves. The anointed priest enacts expiation *(kipper)* for the sanctuary, the tent, the altar, the priests, and all the people of the assembly. The enactment of the ritual is an everlasting statute (cf. the occurrence of this phrase in 3:17; 7:36; 10:9; 16:29-34; 17:7; 23:14, 21, 31, 41; 24:3). The ritual process narrated in this text conforms to Yahweh's instructions (v. 34).

THE HOLINESS CODE
Leviticus 17–26

Leviticus 17–26 is generally recognized as a distinct collection of materials that emphasize the call for the Israelite community to be holy (the holiness code). These chapters focus more on social interaction and social enactment than do the first sixteen chapters. This is, of course, a matter of emphasis. Leviticus 17–26 also reflect significant ritual concerns, and chs. 1–16, significant social concerns.

In Lev. 17–26, the focus is on how the Israelite community is to enact holiness. Holiness is understood primarily in relational terms. The community actualizes its holiness as it enacts just social relations. In addition, the enacted holiness of the community is a reflection of the holiness of Yahweh. In this way, the holiness of Yahweh itself comes to be seen in relational terms. Holiness is not an abstract quality, nor is it the "separation" of Yahweh from the community. It is a relational category that comes into being in, by, and through enacted relationships based on justice, integrity, honesty, and faithfulness.

SACRIFICE AND BLOOD (CH. 17)

Leviticus 17 serves as the introduction to the holiness code. It has two primary concerns: (1) the sacrificial slaughter and presentation of animals (vv. 2-9) and (2) the prohibition against human consumption of animal blood (see vv. 4, 10, 11, 12, 13, 14; cf. Gen. 9:4-6; Lev. 3:17). The structure of the chapter is important for its interpretation (see Milgrom 1971; Gorman 1990, 181-89; Schwartz 1991). The instructions are delivered to

Moses, who is to pass them on to the whole community (cf. Lev. 21:24; 22:18).

The recurring phrase "if anyone from the house of Israel" (vv. 3, 8, 10, 13) introduces the major units of the chapter. Each unit contains the *karet* penalty (vv. 4, 9, 10, 14; see 7:19-21), and the instructions introduced in vv. 3, 8, and 13 include motivational or explanatory material. The instructional unit that begins in v. 13 concludes at v. 14 with the general statement of the *karet* penalty. Verse 15 begins a new instructional unit ("all persons who eat"). Thus, excluding the introductory statement, there are five basic instructional units in ch. 17: vv. 3-7, 8-9, 10-12, 13-14, and 15-16.

Unit One (vv. 3-7)

In vv. 3-7, the primary ruling states that any Israelite who slaughters an ox, a lamb, or a goat, either inside or outside the camp, must present it at the entrance of the tent as an offering to Yahweh. Failure to do this constitutes blood-guilt, the guilt associated with the shedding of innocent blood. Any person who contracts blood-guilt will be cut off *(karet)*. This statement appears to contradict Deut. 12:15-16, which only requires that the blood be poured out on the ground. The larger context of Lev. 17:3-7, however, indicates that verses 3-5 refer specifically to the sacrificial slaughter of the offerings of well-being. In addition, the word used for "slaughter" *(shahat)* consistently refers to "sacrificial" slaughter in the priestly traditions (Milgrom 1991, 713-18). Thus, the well-being sacrifices must be presented at the tent. Failure to do so results in blood-guilt. A sacrificial animal whose blood is not manipulated by a priest is viewed as a victim of murder; the one who slaughters it is guilty of murder (cf. Genesis 9:1-7) and is subject to the *karet* penalty (see Lev. 7:19-21 on the *karet* penalty).

Verses 5-7 prohibit the improper worship of pagan deities. The Israelites must present their sacrifices of well-being at the tent; in so doing they cannot offer them to other gods. This guarantees that the sacrificial blood is thrown on the altar and that the animal fat is burned by a priest. These verses reinforce the proper place and manner of sacrifice.

101

Unit Two (vv. 8-9)

Verses 8-9 provide two additional rulings. First, the non-Israelites who dwell with Israel *(ger)* are now included in the instructions. Second, the ruling is extended to the burnt offerings. In this way, the concern of the text broadens. Both the well-being offerings and the burnt offerings must be brought to the tent. Failure to do so results in the *karet* penalty.

Unit Three (vv. 10-12)

Verses 10-12 stand at the center of the chapter. There is an initial ruling combined with the *karet* penalty (v. 10). An explanatory verse follows that includes three basic statements: (a) the life of the flesh is in the blood; (b) Yahweh has given the blood so that it might be placed on the altar for "expiation" *(kipper);* and (c) it is the blood, in terms of life, that accomplishes expiation. A restatement and expansion of the initial statement forms the conclusion.

Verse 10 indicates that the unit deals generally with *all* animal blood and not of any one specific sacrifice: "if anyone . . . eats *any* blood." Two reasons are provided to explain the prohibition. First, the blood is not to be eaten because the life of the animal is in the blood (v. 11a). Although the text does not explicitly state that life is sacred or that it belongs to God, it is probable that the priests would have attached sacred significance to the life in the blood.

Second, the blood has been given by God to be placed on the altar for the ritual enactment of expiation (v. 11b). The blood is not to be consumed because it has a ritual use. The reason for this statement, however, forms the crux of the interpretive problem: "because the blood, by the life, will expiate" (v. 11c). Two questions arise: (1) What actually serves to bring about expiation, and (2) how does it actually do it?

Three basic views have been proposed for the key phrase, "by the life" (v. 11c). First, it is the life in the blood that actually accomplishes and effects expiation (instrumental). Second, the life of the animal is given in exchange for expiation (the payment of a price). Third, it is a restatement of the matter, "it is the blood, as life;" the two phrases say the same thing. This places a great deal of interpretive weight on a single proposition.

The association of the blood with the life is made twice in v. 11. The blood expiates because of the life that is in it. Emphasis is placed on the ritual use of the life in the blood. The manipulation of the (life in the) blood, *in the context of ritual,* expiates on behalf of the Israelites.

The meaning one assigns to the word *kipper* is critical. There are two basic views (for reviews, see Milgrom 1991, 1079-84; Hartley 1992, 63-66). First, it may be related to *kopher,* which means "ransom." In this view, the life in the blood is placed on the altar to provide a ransom or a substitute for the life of the offerer. The precise reason for such a ransom is unclear. Some argue it is payment for sin, whereas others believe it is a payment for the life of the slaughtered animal. Second, *kipper* often means to "cleanse," "purge," or "wipe away." In this view, the blood placed on the altar cleanses impurities (i.e., the blood of the purification offering). This does not explain, however, why 17:10-12 emphasizes the "life" in the blood rather than its ability to absorb. The tendency has been to seek a single, all-inclusive meaning. In that vv. 10-12 present a *general* statement, it is better to assign to *kipper* a more general sense. The life of an animal is in its blood, and the blood has been "set apart" to address a wide range of problems having to do with sin, trespass, and impurity.

Thus, it is the expiatory power of the ritual process that is emphasized in this text. The manipulation of the blood effects expiation. That is the primary reason for the blood prohibition. The reason it is effective in ritual is because it is "charged" with the life of the animal. In addition, it is probable that the text prohibits the consumption of blood because the life of the animal is considered sacred.

Unit Four (vv. 13-14)

Verses 13-14 address the question of animal blood in relation to hunting. There is a basic ruling (v. 13) and an explanation for it (v. 14). In the explanatory statement, the association of the life of an animal and its blood connects this unit to the previous one. The blood of an animal or bird killed for food must be poured out on the ground and covered with earth (v. 13). The explanation follows: "because the life of all flesh, its blood is bound up with its life" (v. 14). This is a restatement of the notion that the life of an animal is in its blood (vv. 10-12). Yahweh has prohibited the consumption of blood precisely because the life of an animal is in its blood. Any person who eats it will be "cut off."

The pouring out of the blood is best understood as an act of reverence that demonstrates respect for the life of the animal and, thus, respect for God, who created and continues to care for that life. It is a hunting ritual that is enjoined on the Israelites and is distinct from, but related to, the rulings on Israel's ritual activity in relation to the altar. In pouring out the blood, the hunter "presents" the life of the animal to Yahweh.

Unit Five (vv. 15-16)

Verses 15-16 do not contain a prohibition. They recognize and assume that people will eat animals that are found in the wild. Eating such animals makes one unclean, but purification is easily accomplished: launder clothes, bathe in water, and wait until evening (v. 15). The more serious problem, however, arises if a person fails to follow these instructions. Such a person "must bear the guilt" associated with the act (v. 16). The concern is for the continued state of impurity and the ongoing refusal to enact a purification ritual. The phrase "to bear the guilt" is equivalent to the *karet* penalty (see 7:19-21).

THE FAMILY AND SEXUAL RELATIONS (CH. 18)

Leviticus 18 reflects a variety of concerns and an interesting mix of material. Parenetic material — "preached instruction" or "sermonic calls to obedience" — opens (vv. 2-5) and closes (vv. 24-30) the chapter. Parenesis provides reasons for obedience. In ch. 18, "law" and "proclamation" are interactive and mutually supportive. One begins to hear an ethical tone that has been largely, although not entirely, absent up to this point in Leviticus.

These instructions attempt to construct a model for various prohibited and, therefore, by implication, permitted sexual partners and activity in the context of the Israelite family. The instructions reflect the social, cultural, and theological views of one "group" (the Holiness school) within Israel. It is not certain whether these views reflect a theoretical construct of the way things ought to be or whether they reflect actual social practice. It is probably a combination of the two. It is important to recognize the ancient social, cultural, and historical contexts that shaped this chapter's views on sexual activity and the family.

Chapter 18 demonstrates the close theological relationship that ritual/ceremonial instructions have with moral/ethical instructions. This chapter has a significant number of linguistic and conceptual relationships to the instructions on ritual and purity found elsewhere in Leviticus. For Israel, the instructions of Yahweh are of a single piece and have equal validity. In Leviticus, radical distinctions between ritual and ethical instructions do not hold.

The chapter constitutes both a social *and* theological statement; the two are inseparable. Chapter 18 thus contributes to the construction of a social-theological world of meaning within which the Israelites locate themselves and enact their lives (see Frymer-Kensky 1989, 91-95). These traditions reflect a deep concern for matters associated with the body and recognize the physical nature of human life and existence. Sexuality is one significant aspect of a "bodied" existence.

Excluding the opening introductory formula (v. 1-2a), the chapter consists of four parts: an opening parenetic statement (vv. 2-5); instructions identifying prohibited sexual partners (vv. 6-18); instructions identifying prohibited sexual activity (vv. 19-23); and concluding parenetic material (vv. 24-30).

Opening Statement (vv. 2-5)

The introductory parenetic statement calls on Israel to obey the instructions that follow. The divine self-identification formula — "I am Yahweh" or "I am Yahweh your God" — occurs three times (vv. 2b, 4b, 5b). Yahweh, the God of Israel, stands at the heart of the call to obedience. Two ways of life are contrasted: the way of the other nations (the land of Egypt and the land of Canaan are specified) and the way prescribed for Israel by Yahweh. Israel's life is significantly related to its history. Israel is not to do as the residents of the land of Egypt, *where you lived,* nor is Israel to do as they do in the land of Canaan, *to which I am bringing you.* Located in the wilderness, these words look back to Israel's past history in Egypt and forward to Israel's future history in the land of Canaan. They emphasize Yahweh's presence in the life of the community as it moves from slavery to freedom. The divine presence is itself a call to obedience.

Sexual Partners (vv. 6-18)

The instructions in verses 6-18 attempt to structure family identity in terms of sexual relationships. The text structures society along patrilineal and patriarchal lines. The family was structured in terms of specified relations to the "father," and the male perspective provides the normative point of view (see Rattray 1987; Levine 1989, 117-18, 253-55).

Two basic types of relations are specified (Levine 1989, 117). The first is expressed in terms of "flesh" relations and has to do with those who are related through blood and birth. The second is expressed in terms of "nakedness" and has to do with relations established through marriage. "To uncover the nakedness" is a euphemism for sexual intercourse, which functions to bind together partners. Thus, a woman's nakedness is said to be the nakedness of her husband. The chapter defines "the family" in terms of sexual activity in order to maintain the integrity of the family. The instructions construct an order of relationships that is integral to the larger orders of society, cult, and cosmos (Frymer-Kensky 1989, 97-98).

The unit opens with a general statement: "No one shall approach a person who is near of kin ('flesh of your flesh') to uncover nakedness (i.e., to have sexual intercourse): I am Yahweh" (v. 6). Various implications of this general guideline are detailed in vv. 7-18. Persons who are "near of kin" include mother, father, son, daughter, brother, virgin sister, and, for the nonpriest, wife (see

21:2-3; Rattray 1987). A second general statement is found in v. 7: "The nakedness of your father, that is, the nakedness of your mother, you must not uncover; she is your mother, you must not uncover her nakedness." Two principles are operative. First, the father and the mother stand as the two primary points of reference, and the remainder of the list develops in relationship to these two people. Second, it is stated that the nakedness of the father is the nakedness of the mother (Bigger 1979, 196-97; Levine 1989, 120). Sexual activity with the mother is considered equivalent to sexual activity with the father. This is a relationship established by marriage. The remainder of the list defines the ways a man and a woman can become one flesh through sexual activity.

The following persons are prohibited as sexual partners (see Rattray 1987): one's stepmother ("the nakedness of the father's wife," v. 8); one's half-sister (v. 9); one's granddaughters (v. 10); one's stepsister (a child of one's father and stepmother, v. 11); one's aunt (the father's sister, v. 12, and the mother's sister, v. 13); the wife of the father's brother (aunt by marriage, v. 14); one's daughter-in-law (v. 15); the wife of one's brother (v. 16); a woman and her daughter (v. 17a); a step-granddaughter (v. 17b); a sister-in-law while the sister is alive (v. 18). Those who are prohibited on the basis of "nakedness" (i.e., because of the bond that exists between sexual partners) are: mother (v. 7), stepmother (v. 8), granddaughter (v. 10), and brother's wife (v. 16). Those that are prohibited on the basis of "flesh" relations are: father's sister (v. 12), mother's sister (v. 13), and step-granddaughter (v. 17). Some exclusions are explained simply by stating the relationship: for example, father's wife's daughter, "since she is your sister" (v. 11). There are some surprising omissions in the list: daughter, full sister (unless indicated and assumed in v. 9), grandmother, and wife of the mother's brother. Their prohibited status, however, may be deduced on the basis of the existing list and is assumed.

Sexual Activity (vv. 19-23)

Verses 19-23 reflect a different concern but are included at this point because of verbal and thematic similarities with vv. 2-28.

These verses, with the exception of the Molech statement (v. 21), constitute a series of prohibitions against certain types of sexual activity. The common concern is "wasted seed." They identify a group of activities that cannot produce and maintain children within the socially approved family (Eilberg-Schwartz 1990, 177-94).

Verse 19 prohibits sexual relations with a woman while she is in her menstrual impurity (cf. 20:18 and 15:19-24). Such impurity is communicated through sexual intercourse. The activity is prohibited not just because of the risk of impurity but because it cannot be expected to produce children (Eilberg-Schwartz 1990, 182-86). For the priestly traditionists, acceptable sexual activity should lead to conception.

Verse 20 prohibits sexual relations with the wife of one's neighbor. Adultery is prohibited elsewhere in the Pentateuch (e.g., Exod. 20:14, 17; Deut. 5:18). The prohibitions against adultery are written from a male perspective, although the consequences of such activity are brought to bear on both persons involved. The prohibition against adultery reflects the priestly understanding of the husband-wife relationship, which incorporates faithfulness in sexual relations. This relationship reflects, to some degree, the stories of creation. Male and female together make up the image of God (Gen. 1:27); procreation is part of God's blessing. The integrity of the marriage relationship must be protected. In addition, any children that might result from adultery would not be considered legitimate children of the family.

Verse 21 prohibits offering children to Molech because it profanes the name of God (cf. Lev. 20:2-5). It is followed by the divine self-identification formula. The presence of this prohibition within this series is somewhat puzzling. Although the evidence is not conclusive at present, it appears that the cult of Molech included the sacrifice of children, ancestral worship, and worship of the dead (Heider 1985, 232-73, 383-408; Day 1989, 4-28). It is not clear if it was a popular form of religion practiced by the people of the land or whether it was a form of elitist worship practiced by rulers. In either case, the sacrifice of children to Molech not only breaks the prohibition against worshipping other gods (Exod. 20:3) but also runs counter to the blessing of creation in that it destroys the life of the child. Thus, the worship of Molech posed a threat to "the seed" of the Israelites.

Verse 22 prohibits lying with a man as with a woman and terms this act an "abomination" *(to'ebah)*. The present priestly context prohibits such activity because it cannot produce children. It constitutes an act of "wasted seed" (Bigger 1979, 202-3; Eilberg-Schwartz 1990, 182-86). This is true for two reasons. First, one must account for its inclusion in a series that includes the prohibition against Molech worship. Molech worship killed "the seed." Second, there is no parallel prohibition for women (possibly a result of the male-centered perspective of the text, although v. 23 suggests otherwise). The present context is more concerned with the *consequence* of sexual activity than with the activity itself. The concern is with the loss of the male seed in nonfertile activity. The concern is not the morality of sexual activity but the pragmatics of producing children.

Finally, verse 23 prohibits sexual activity with animals for both men and women. This constitutes "confusion" *(tebel)* because it reflects an improper crossing of boundaries between the human realm and the animal realm. The good order of creation establishes a categorical distinction between human beings and animals (Gen. 1:24-28) that must remain intact. There is also evidence that some of Israel's neighbors practiced bestiality. Thus, this prohibition stands against pagan practices, wasted seed, and the violation of the boundary that separates humans and animals.

The divine directive to be fruitful and multiply provides the common focus of these instructions (Gen. 1:28). The concern is to maximize the fertile use of the male seed. Clearly, the normative "point of view" is patriarchal. It should also be recognized that the Israelites did not know and understand the precise biological processes involved in conception and birth.

Each of the statements is deeply embedded in the literary, historical, social, cultural, and ideological contexts of ancient Israel. Simple and immediate appropriation (i.e., "application") of these statements to contemporary society must be avoided. The ancient context and the contemporary context are not the same. In addition, these prohibitions are significant elements of the priestly *ritual* system. For the priestly traditionists, these instructions were all important parts of a single system that included a specific vision and understanding of the world. Each expression of that system had equal validity and weight — one cannot pick and choose to enforce one and ignore another. The instructions must always be understood in the context of the priestly world view. Finally, the priestly traditionists sought to *affirm* human life and existence within the context of the Israelite community. These statements reflect a view of community as expressed by one set of traditions, which are not a full, final, or normative statement for all times and all places.

Concluding Statement (vv. 24-30)

The parenetic speech that closes the chapter (vv. 24-30) emphasizes the relationship that exists between the life of Israel and its life on the land. Israel must avoid the defilement associated with the prohibited practices (v. 24). The nations in the land before Israel's arrival defiled themselves with such practices; the land became defiled and "vomited" them out (v. 25). The relationship between the land and its inhabitants is emphasized elsewhere in the holiness code (e.g., 20:22-26; 26). This relationship is also discussed in nonpriestly texts (e.g., Hos. 4:1-3; Jer. 4:23-26).

Another tradition accuses the people of the land of improper sexual activity. For example, Ham, the father of Canaan, is accused of "seeing the nakedness" of his father Noah. The result is that "Canaan" is cursed and made the slave of his brothers (Gen. 9:20-27). Similar themes are also present in the story of the origins of the Moabites and Ammonites (Gen. 19:30-38). These stories may have functioned, in part, to provide a moral basis for Israel's conquest of the land (although a contemporary reading must raise questions about the moral status of such moral rationalizations). Israel remembers its history with the people of the land in terms of political, military, and economic conflict and struggle (e.g., the story of Esau and Jacob in Gen. 25:19-33), and its depiction of Canaan and the other people of the land must thus be understood within this context. Since it is not uncommon to emphasize the negative aspects of one's enemies, it is not surprising that Israel used negative moral evaluations of its enemies to rationalize, justify, and motivate its struggles with them. The priestly traditionists drew on these negative traditions in their call for Israel to worship only Yahweh. Contemporary readers must recognize the dangers of caricature and prejudice in these traditional constructions of the "other folk" who are "not like us."

The chapter concludes with a warning that the land will also "vomit" Israel out if it practices abominable and defiling activities. Indeed, anyone who practices such acts will be "cut off" *(karet)*. Israel must keep itself separate from the nations through the way it lives its life on the land. The speech closes with the divine self-identification formula: "I am Yahweh your God."

MISCELLANEOUS INSTRUCTIONS (CH. 19)

Leviticus 19 consists of a series of miscellaneous instructions. Both ritual and social matters are included in the call for the community to practice holiness. A number of parallels exist between this chapter and the decalogue in Exod. 20. Both texts include a call to honor and revere one's parents, to observe the sabbath, to avoid idolatry and the worship of other gods, to avoid stealing and related forms of deceitful conduct, and to avoid false oaths. A few prophetic texts refer to these same matters (e.g., Hos. 4:2; Jer. 7:5-8). This indicates that priests, prophets, and lawmakers agreed on certain "rulings" in their reflections on the Yahweh-Israel relationship and the practice of community.

The chapter opens with a call for the community to be holy (v. 2), a central concern of the holiness code. It is related to Yahweh's call for Israel to be "a priestly community and a holy nation" in the context of the Sinai covenant (Exod. 19:4-6). Israel is to manifest holiness, justice, and integrity in its own life and in its life with the world (see Fretheim 1991, 208-14; Dozeman 1989, 93-98).

Holiness takes on a relational and experiential meaning; it is not just a quality or power associated with the divine being. In Lev. 19, holiness is enacted and actualized in, by, and through the life of the community. The divine life, understood in relational terms, is paradigmatic for Israel's life. Holiness is manifest in relationships characterized by integrity, honesty, faithfulness, and love. The call for Israel to be holy is the call for the community to concretize the divine life in the world. Holiness is actualized in the context of the community as it manifests the life of God.

The divine self-identification formula occurs repeatedly in the chapter: "I am Yahweh" (vv. 12b, 14b, 16b, 18b, 28b, 30b, 32b, 37b) or "I am Yahweh your God" (vv. 3b, 4b, 10b, 25b, 31b, 34b, 36b). In this context, the phrase emphasizes that the instructions are grounded in the divine life. The divine life is present within the instructions, and it will be concretized as the community observes these instructions. For practical issues, the self-identification formula will be used to structure the discussion of this chapter.

Verses 2b-4 contain four basic statements. The initial call to be holy, (v. 2), a call to revere ("fear") one's mother and father (v. 3a), a call to keep the sabbaths of Yahweh (v. 3b), and a prohibition against the making of idols and images (v. 4). The opening call to holiness provides the primary context for these foundational statements. The first statement emphasizes the importance of the family for social order. The second emphasizes the importance of sabbath observance (ritual enactment). It provides a temporal order for social and cultic life in Israel. The third emphasizes the exclusive worship that Yahweh desires and demands from this community. Family life, ritual, and worship of Yahweh are interwoven; they are elements of the life of holiness.

Verses 5-10 contain two distinct instructional statements. The first (vv. 5-8) states that the sacrifices of well-being (cf. Lev. 3 and 7:11-18) must be eaten on the first or second day. If eaten on the third day, the effectiveness of the sacrifice is negated. The eating of the sacrificial food is a crucial element of the ritual process. Any person who eats the meat improperly is subject to punishment (the *karet* penalty) because such activity profanes the holy (see 7:19-27).

The second issue (vv. 9-10) has to do with harvesting and reflects a concern for the poor in society. This ruling relates to the previous one through a common concern for "eating." The Israelites are to leave the edges of their fields unharvested and to leave the gleanings in the fields. They are not to strip their vineyards or gather fallen grapes. These are to go to the poor and the non-Israelites who dwell within the community. The holy community must care for the poor in its midst.

Verses 11-12 contain four instructional statements. Israel is not to steal, deal falsely, lie, or swear falsely using God's name. The community must practice integrity and honesty in relationships. People must speak and act honestly and in good faith in their dealings with other persons in the community. To swear falsely in God's name is to profane the name of God (cf. 18:21). In effect, swearing falsely in God's name makes God an accomplice to the lie (cf. 6:1-7). The practice of integrity and honesty are at the heart of the practice and experience of holiness.

Verses 13-14 continue the call for social integrity and contain six instructional statements. The first three are closely related to the directions in vv. 11-12. The Israelites must not defraud their neighbors. Specifically, they must not cheat each other in matters relating to goods or possessions. Stealing is prohibited. The Israelites must respect the rights of others to have and maintain possession of their own goods. The laborer is to be paid on the day that services are rendered; wages are not to be withheld until the morning. This statement is directed at those in a position of power who hire day workers. Holiness demands a demonstrated concern for the poor and powerless.

Verse 14 contains three statements. The first two are more proverbial than legal: Do not revile the deaf or put a stumbling block before the blind. Taken literally, these statements require the community to respect those who are deaf or blind. If proverbial, however, the statements prohibit any attempt to harm another person because of or on the basis of limited capabilities. If the latter view is correct, these statements constitute a call to act compassionately when dealing with other persons. The unit concludes with a call to fear God.

Verses 15-16 consist of six instructional statements. They constitute a call for the Israelites to practice justice in personal relationships. Justice is an enacted social relation, a social practice. The ritual enactment of order is intimately connected to the social enactment of justice.

The first four statements refer to legal proceedings: (a) do not act unjustly in judgment, (b) do not be partial to the poor, (c) do not show favor to the great, and (d) judge your neighbor with justice. They call for just judgments that are not influenced by a person's status. Legal judgments must be based on evidence and testimony and must respect the rights of the persons involved in the case. For the holiness code the question is not, "What is the right thing to do?" Rather, it calls for the people to "do that which they know to be right."

The final two statements indicate that an Israelite is not to gain an advantage — economic, judicial, or social — at the cost of an innocent person. Slander is not permitted because it harms another person. Neither can one "stand against the blood" of a neighbor. This phrase indicates that one must not act in a way that is harmful to another person — either in business, in court, in social contexts, or in the home.

Verses 17-18 contain four instructional statements that focus on interpersonal and social relations. The first prohibits the Israelites from hating ("with their hearts") any of their kin. The second requires that they reprove a neighbor who is doing wrong or run the risk of incurring guilt themselves. These two statements are similar. To hate a person is, in some sense, to "stand against" that person. To reprove a person is, in some sense, to "stand with" that person. The Israelites must "stand together" in their effort to embody the instructions of Yahweh within the community. Failure to attempt to stop another person's damaging activity is to accept that activity and, in effect, to approve it. "Doing nothing" is clearly seen as "doing something." The third statement prohibits the Israelites from taking vengeance, bearing grudges, or seeking to retaliate against others. The fourth statement calls for the Israelites to love their neighbors as they love themselves. In this context, love is a means of relating to and interacting with other persons. The larger context for this call to love is the vision of a just community, a community that manifests the holiness of God through its life. Love has to do with social practice that is based on integrity, honesty, and respect.

Verses 19-25 may be divided into three basic parts. First, v. 19 prohibits (1) the breeding of two distinct kinds of animals, (2) the sowing of a field with two kinds of seeds, and (3) the wearing of a garment made of two types of materials (cf. Deut. 22:9-11;

Carmichael 1982). These instructions reflect the priestly desire to maintain the basic categories of creation (cf. Lev. 10:10). Creation becomes the context for everyday expressions of life, and everyday life becomes a means of enacting the order of creation. In this way, the Israelites reflect the holiness of God!

Second, vv. 20-22 describe a situation in which the marriage price of a female slave has been arranged but another man has had sexual relations with her before the husband-to-be has paid the woman's owner. A payment must be made (so Speiser 1960, 34; Wenham 1979, 270-71; and Levine 1989, 130-31; but cf. Milgrom 1977 and Schwartz 1986), but the couple is not to be put to death because the woman is still a slave (cf. Deut. 22:23-29; Exod. 21:7-11). The man who had relations with her must present a ram as a reparation offering because the act is viewed as a form of adultery. The payment plus the reparation offering bring about forgiveness (see Milgrom 1977). The economic rights of the owner of the slave are the primary concern in this ruling.

Third, vv. 23-25 prohibit eating the fruit of trees for the first three years after their planting. The "foreskin" of the tree must be left on it for the first three years. In this time, the fruit is not to be eaten and the tree is not to be pruned. During this time, the tree is "unfruitful" because it is "uncircumcised." In the fourth year, the fruit is set aside for God, and only in the fifth year may Israel eat of it. The pruning of fruit trees and circumcision, the rite by which a male becomes a member of the covenant community, are related in this text (see Eilberg-Schwartz 1990, 141-76). This "sacred" ruling may reflect the pragmatics of effective horticulture.

Verses 26-28 contain four instructional statements. They prohibit practices associated with pagan cultic activities. The first prohibition states, "you shall not eat on/over the blood." This phrasing is distinct from the blood prohibitions in Gen. 9:4 and Lev. 3:17 and 17:10-14. This statement is concerned with a non-Israelite (= pagan) cultic practice involving the consumption of animal blood (Levine 1989, 132-33). The phrase is found in the story of Saul's troops eating "on the blood" after a military victory (1 Sam. 14:31-35). The context of the Leviticus ruling suggests that a pagan practice is intended.

The second statement prohibits witchcraft and soothsaying (v. 26b), both of which are associated with pagan efforts to interact with the "sacred" realm. The third prohibition states that a man must not round off the hair of his temples nor mar the edges of his beard (v. 27), practices associated with rituals of mourning the dead (Levine 1989, 133). Finally, Israelites are prohibited from gashing their flesh or marking it (v. 28). The gashing of the flesh is associated with pagan sacrifice (see 1 Kings 18:28). Thus, all four statements in vv. 26-28 prohibit pagan cultic practices.

Verses 29-30 contain two statements. The first prohibits a man from profaning his daughter by making her a prostitute; such activity pollutes and defiles the land itself. Clearly, the actions of the people have consequences for the land (cf. Lev. 18:24-30). Family relationships, particularly in matters relating to sexual activity, were believed to have a close connection to the life of the land (cf. ch. 18). This connection is made, it would appear, because each is concerned to some degree with fertility. The ruling does not provide the viewpoint of the daughter. It seeks to prohibit a specific activity by the father, but the motivation is a concern for the land. The voice of the woman remains silent in this ruling.

The second statement calls for Israel to keep the sabbaths of Yahweh and to revere ("fear") the sanctuary (cf. v. 3). Both attitude and action are involved in Israel's manifestation of the sanctity and holiness of both sabbath and temple. "To keep" (ritual activity) and "to fear" (reverent attitude) are interconnected means for living in the context of the holy.

Verse 31 prohibits Israel from seeking information from ghosts and spirits associated with the earth and the dead. This prohibition has foreign cultic and religious practices in mind. Such "inquiring" is an affront to Yahweh, who speaks with the Israelites.

Verse 32 instructs the Israelites to stand in the presence of the aged and to defer to the elderly. This reflects the proverbial tradition that believes wisdom comes with age and experience (e.g., Prov. 16:31; 20:29). Israel respected the elders of the community and affirmed their value within and for the community.

Verses 33-34 address the treatment of "the resident stranger."

The "stranger" (*ger*) is not of Israelite descent, but lives and works with and among the Israelites. Such people would include merchants and craftspersons (see van Houten 1991, 109-57). They are to be treated as real citizens of the community ("you shall love them as yourself"; cf. v. 18), and they are not to be oppressed. The basis for this ruling is Israel's own experience in Egypt.

Verses 35-37 bring the chapter to a close. Two parallel instructional statements focus on honest measures in business. The divine call to be holy includes honesty and integrity in business dealings. Indeed, holiness requires that honesty, integrity, and faithfulness be practiced in all areas of life.

The chapter concludes by recalling that Yahweh brought Israel out of Egypt and renews the call to be obedient. Yahweh has acted and seeks a community that will act in response to the divine action. The chapter closes with the self-identification formula: "I am Yahweh."

MISCELLANEOUS INSTRUCTIONS (CH. 20)

The instructions in Lev. 20 cover a variety of issues that are directed at the whole community (vv. 1-2a) and continue the instructions found in chs. 18–19. Chapter 20 places more emphasis on the punishments and penalties to be rendered for disobedience. The penalties indicate that the community is responsible, to a large extent, for caring for itself. The text does indicate situations in which Yahweh will punish the guilty party, but, repeatedly, emphasis is placed on the responsibility of the community.

Verses 1-6 open the instructions with a statement prohibiting the worship of Molech (cf. 18:21). Both Israelites and "the resident strangers" (see 19:33-34) are to be put to death if they offer a child to Molech (see 18:21). It is the responsibility of the people to stone them to death. In addition, Yahweh promises to execute the *karet* penalty (v. 3a; see 7:19-21). Punishment includes both the death penalty (the community) and extermination of the lineage (Yahweh). If the people fail to execute judgment, God will not (vv. 4-5).

In the same way, the Israelites are warned against turning to spirits or ghosts (cf. 19:31). Both Molech worship and "turning to" ghosts and spirits are characterized as "prostitution" (*zanah*; vv. 5, 6). These are acts of faithlessness, in which the guilty party turns from Yahweh to other gods and religious practices. Both activities constitute a form of cultic practice associated with spirits of the earth and the worship of ancestors (Levine 1989, 136-37). In addition, the worship of spirits and ancestors is viewed as a confusion of categories — the line between the living and the dead is dangerously crossed (note the juxtaposition of the "seed" and the "dead").

Verses 7-8 open with a parenetic call to holiness, which leads to a list of punishments for improper sexual activity. The divine life and holiness must be reflected in the life of the community. The self-identification formula — "I am Yahweh who sanctifies (*meqaddishkem*) you" (v. 8) — introduces a call to obedience. Yahweh and the people share in the construction of a holy community: "I am the one who sanctifies you; sanctify yourselves!"

Verse 9 declares that all who curse their father or mother are to be put to death (cf. the call "to revere mother and father" in 19:3). The "cursing" of parents is viewed as an act of violence. Although the community must punish such a person, it will not become guilty for shedding the guilty party's blood (Hartley 1992, 338-39). This statement relates to the following instructions through the phrase, "their blood is upon them" (see vv. 11, 12, 13, 16), and through a concern for the constitution of the family.

Verses 10-21 identify the punishments to be rendered against those who engage in prohibited sexual activity. This list is not a precise parallel to the list in ch. 18. Both the order and the specific cases discussed are different. The prescribed punishments, however, provide a basic conceptual structure: vv. 10-16 call for the death penalty, vv. 17-19 invoke the *karet* penalty, and vv. 20-21 result in childlessness.

Verses 10-16 detail seven violations that call for the community to enforce the death penalty against offenders. Included in the list are adultery (v. 10), sexual activity with one's stepmother (v. 11), sexual activity with a daughter-in-law (v. 12), a man who lies with a male as with a woman (v. 13), sexual activity with one's mother-in-law (punished by burning both persons, v. 14), and bestiality (v. 15, 16). In addition, the phrase "their blood is upon them" is found in the cases involving the stepmother (v. 11), the daughter-in-law (v. 12), the males (v. 13), and bestiality with regard to a woman (v. 16). Sexual activity with a daughter-in-law is said to be an act of "confusion" (*tebel;* v. 12), the activity of two males is termed an abomination (*to'ebah;* v. 13), and sexual activity with a mother-in-law is "depravity" (*zimah;* v. 14).

The priestly effort to construct a system of sexual partners supported by such a severe set of penalties must be understood within two distinct but interrelated contexts. First, the priestly traditions seek to construct a normative social order by defining categories that must be observed. Confusion of the categories results in a disruption of the social order. Only activity that leads to the creation of children who are "legitimate" is approved (see 18:19-23). Second, the priestly traditions seek to maintain the boundary between the realm of life and the realm of death. Sexual activity has to do with the creation of life, and, in the priestly view, the creation of life brings one close to the boundary between life and death.

Caution must be exercised in any effort to "appropriate" these rulings for contemporary life. These statements are deeply embedded in the larger system of priestly ritual and instructions on purity and impurity. The attempt to declare a single ruling as normative "for all times and all places" without, at the same time, accepting the whole system, fails to understand the historical context of both Israel and the contemporary interpreter. Thus, contemporary discussions that draw on this text to speak of the "sin" of homosexuality fail on two levels. First, they fail to recognize and accept the larger priestly theological, ritual, and purity systems of which these statements are a part. Second, they often fail to recognize that adultery, for example, calls for the death penalty. If contemporary readers are to understand these statements both culturally and theologically, they must recognize and respect the distinctions between the cultural context of ancient Israel and the contemporary cultural context.

Verses 17-21 reflect a chiastic structure, with the general statement "you shall not uncover the nakedness of" (v. 19) at the center. The rulings are written from a male perspective although both the man *and* the woman bear the consequences of the prohibited activities. Verse 17 states that if a man "takes" the daughter of his father or of his mother and they see each other's nakedness, then they are both to be cut off in the sight of the people. Verse 18 states that if a man and woman have sexual relations while she is menstruating, they are to be cut off from their people. Verse 19 states that if a man has sexual activity with an aunt, they both must bear their sin and experience the consequences of their action. Verse 20 states that if a man has sexual relations with his brother's wife, both the man and the woman must bear their *impurity*. He has uncovered the nakedness of his brother; the guilty couple shall die childless. Finally, verse 21 states that a man who marries his brother's wife while his brother is still alive has uncovered his brother's nakedness; the guilty couple will die childless.

Verses 22-26 form a parenetic conclusion to this chapter and states theologically what it means for Israel to be a holy people. It speaks of Israel's relationship to the land and reflects the priestly concern for maintaining the separation of clean and unclean, holy and common. Israel is to keep the statutes and ordinances so that the land to which God is bringing them will not "vomit" them out (v. 22). The nations that are being driven out did these things, and God abhorred them (v. 23; cf. 18:24-30).

Verse 24 contains both a promise and a declaration and has three basic parts. It opens with a reminder of the promise that Israel will inherit the land. This is followed by the divine self-identification formula "I am Yahweh your God," coupled with a declarative statement "and I have 'separated' you from the peoples." Promise moves to and is grounded in self-declaration, which serves as a basis for national identity. Israel's status as a "separated" people is based on God's identity, God's activity, and God's promise.

Verse 25 emphasizes the relationship between Israel's "separation" of the clean and the unclean and Israel's status as a "separated" people. Israel's separation unto God is to be reflected in their separation of the clean from the unclean. This recalls the

120

priestly charge to separate the clean from the unclean, the holy from the common (10:10), as well as the divine acts of separation in creation (Gen. 1). The holiness of the community is ultimately grounded in the very good order of creation.

Verse 26 restates the call to be holy. It gives voice to Israel's understanding of itself as an elect people. It also emphasizes, however, that such "elect" status brings with it the responsibility for the community to reflect the holiness of the divine life.

Verse 27 requires that the community stone to death a person who practices any activity associated with the forbidden realm of the dead or of ghosts (see vv. 1-6).

PRIESTLY AND SACRIFICIAL HOLINESS (CHS. 21–22)

Leviticus 21–22 consist of a series of instructional statements spoken by Yahweh to Moses that cover a variety of issues. The instructions in 21:1–22:15 are directed at the priesthood (see 21:1, 17; 22:2), whereas those in 22:17-30 are addressed more generally to the whole Israelite community (see 22:18). The instructions address cultic matters, although the emphasis continues to be on the community experience and enactment of holiness.

Priestly Purity (21:1-9)

Verses 1b-9 address four issues relating to priestly purity. The first concerns corpse contamination and family. Priests are not allowed to defile themselves in this way except for "blood" relations — relatives who are closely related through birth (see 18:6-18): mother, father, son, daughter, brother, or virgin sister. Although the husband of a married sister would be expected to attend to her burial, priests are not allowed to attend to the burial of their wives. Priests are not responsible to their wives in the same way that nonpriests are expected to be. Later Judaism recognized this ruling to be impractical and allowed the priest to bury his wife (Levine 1989, 142-43).

Verse 5 prohibits priests from participating in rites associated with the dead and in pagan burial rites: shaving their heads, cutting their beards, or gashing themselves (cf. 19:26-28 for a similar prohibition for all Israelites). Verse 6 calls for the priests to be holy because they bring near to the altar the fire offerings of Yahweh. The holiness of the priests is related to their location in the sacred area and their enactment of sacred activity.

Verse 7 prohibits the priests from marrying a woman who practices harlotry, who is defiled, or who has been divorced. The phrase "practices harlotry and is defiled" *(zonah wahalalah)* might be understood as two distinct categories ("a harlot *and* a defiled woman") or two related characteristics ("a woman who has defiled herself *through* such practices") (cf. v. 14 for the same combination). The prohibition reflects the priestly concern for the offspring that she might produce. In this view, a sexually active woman cannot guarantee the paternal status of her children. Similar concerns explain the reason for prohibiting a priest from marrying a divorced woman. Divorce was often related to adultery or sexual impropriety (cf. Deut. 24:1). The central issue is not "morality." The ruling seeks to watch over and maintain the purity of the priestly lineage. Verse 8 restates v. 6. The priesthood is "separated" from the rest of the community through its special status within the realm of the holy. The people must recognize this status.

Verse 9 states that the daughter of a priest who defiles herself as a prostitute (cf. v. 7) profanes her father and is to be burned to death. The ruling applies only to the daughters of priests. This patriarchal ruling reflects the priestly effort to maintain the purity of the priestly lineage.

The High Priest (vv. 10-15)

Verses 10-15 focus on two issues specifically related to the high priest: a general prohibition against corpse contamination and a statement defining acceptable marriage partners. In both cases, rulings for the high priest are more stringent than those for the other priests. The high priest is the one "on whose head the anointing oil was poured" (cf. Lev. 8:12) and who was ordained to "wear the vestments" (cf. Exod. 28). The high priest is not to dishevel his hair, tear his clothing in mourning, or go to a place at which there is a dead body. The high priest is not to go outside the sanctuary *because* the anointing oil is upon him. It makes him holy and *locates* him within the realm of the holy; he shares the holy status of the tabernacle area (see Lev. 8). His departure would disrupt the status of "the holy."

The high priest must marry a woman who has not had previous sexual experience. He may not marry a widow (this prohibition is not included for the ordinary priest), a divorced woman, or a woman defiled through sexual impropriety. He is to marry a virgin of his own kin. The emphasis is on the purity of the priestly line.

"Blemished Priests" (vv. 16-24)

Verses 16-24 state that a member of the priestly family who has a blemish on his body may not "draw near" the altar to offer sacrifices and offerings (vv. 17, 18, 21 [twice], 23). The ruling excludes one who is blind or lame, who has a limb too short or too long (see Levine 1989, 146) or a broken foot or hand, who is a hunchback or a dwarf, who has an eye imperfection, a skin disease (not the unclean skin diseases of Lev. 13, see 22:4), or crushed testicles (vv. 18-20). The wholeness of the body is seen as a reflection of the integrity of the holy. Those who draw near to enact the sacrifices must reflect in the flesh the "wholeness" of the holy realm. Such persons are, however, allowed to eat the food, both the most holy and the holy, that belongs to the priests.

From a contemporary perspective, many of the priestly rulings, and this one is certainly included, are insensitive at best, and reprehensible at worst. It is difficult to reconcile such rulings with an affirmation of the value and integrity of all persons. The above comments emphasize that these rulings must be understood within the context of the larger priestly system of purity and holiness.

Priestly Purity (22:1-9)

Verses 1-9 prohibit the priests, while in a state of impurity, from eating sacred food dedicated by the people. The priests must make certain that their food is treated correctly so as not to profane the name of God. Any priest who comes near to the sacred food while in a state of impurity shall be cut off *(karet)* from the presence of God (v. 3).

The text provides a list of situations that constitute such uncleanness (vv. 4-6). If the priest has an unclean skin eruption (see ch. 13) or a bodily emission (see ch. 15), he cannot eat until he is clean. He may eat only after the complete seven-day ritual of purification is completed (v. 4). If a priest touches anything made unclean by a corpse, by a man who has had an emission of semen, by any swarming thing, or by contact with an unclean person, he becomes unclean and must wait until evening, wash his body, and, one presumes, change his clothing to become clean. Only then may he eat (vv. 5-7). Priests may not eat animals torn by wild beasts or animals that died of natural causes (v. 8).

The concluding verse (v. 9) states that priests must be careful to "keep the charge" given to them by God: to guard the holy place and holy things and to keep them safe from impurities. Failure to do this profanes the sanctuary and makes them guilty. The priests are set apart to maintain the purity of the holy place. If they fail, especially through bringing their own impurity into the sacred area, they are liable to severe judgment; their life is forfeit. This text must be viewed in conjunction with the ordination process (ch. 8). The priests are located in the holy area and mediate between Yahweh and the people, between life and death. They must maintain the integrity of the holy place lest they die. It is dangerous to stand in the holy place!

Eating the Sacrifices and Offerings (vv. 10-16)

Verses 10-16 specify who may and may not eat of the sacred donations. Neither laypersons, bound servants, nor hired laborers are allowed to eat. Slaves of the priests, those bought with silver and those born in the house, are allowed to eat because they are considered part of the household. In that 25:39-44 prohibits making a slave out of an Israelite, the slaves referred to here must be non-Israelites. The daughter of a priest may not eat if she marries a layperson, a nonpriest (v. 12). If, however, she is widowed or divorced and without children, she may return to her father's house and eat of the sacred donations (v. 13).

Verses 14-16 state that if a person unintentionally eats of the sacred food, that person must restore it to the priest along with an additional one-fifth of its value (cf. 5:14-16 for a similar case, which indicates that a reparation offering would also be required). Improper eating of the sacred offerings and sacrifices profanes them. The unit closes with the divine self-identification formula "I am Yahweh," coupled with the declaration "I sanctify them" (v. 16b). This declaration refers to the sacred offerings and sacrifices, which are holy because they are presented and dedicated to God.

Blemished Sacrificial Animals (vv. 17-30)

Verses 17-30 identify acceptable and disqualified sacrificial animals. Sacrificial animals must reflect the holiness of the sacred place. Verses 22-24 specify the "blemishes" that exclude an animal. These physical blemishes parallel, for the most part, those that function to exclude priests from "drawing near" (see 21:18-20).

If a person presents a burnt offering either as payment for a vow or as a freewill offering, the animal must be a male without blemish from the cattle, sheep, or goats. If there is a blemish, it will be unacceptable, and the sacrifice will be ineffective (vv. 17-20).

Verses 21-25 indicate that a sacrifice of well-being, either in payment of a vow or as a freewill sacrifice, must be from the herd or flock and without blemish. An animal is blemished if it is blind, injured, or maimed, or if it has a discharge, an itch, or scabs. An ox or a lamb with a limb either too long or too short may be presented as a freewill sacrifice (v. 23). The exception reflects the fact that a freewill offering is not required; it is a free response to the experience of grace, an enactment of gratitude. Any animal that has its testicles bruised, crushed, torn, or cut must not be offered (v. 24). An animal that is obtained from a foreigner may not be offered because it has been "mutilated" and is, thus, blemished (v. 25). The precise nature of the mutilation is not certain, although this might simply be an effort to prohibit and exclude "foreign" animals from the sacred sacrifices and offerings.

Verses 26-27 prohibit the sacrifice of an ox, sheep, or goat until the eighth day after its birth. It must remain seven days with its mother before it may be slaughtered for sacrifice. This recalls the ruling that a male child is to be circumcised on the eighth day after a seven-day period of purification (12:2-3). The seven-day period represents the normal time for ritual movement from one state to another. This ruling reflects a "separation" rite of sorts, which allows the animal to be temporally and ritually separated from its birth process before its slaughter. The "act of birth" must be separated by at least seven days from the "act of death." The seven days is a temporal means of separating life and death and maintaining the boundary that exists between them.

Verse 28 prohibits the slaughter of an animal and its young on the same day, and the context indicates that the statement refers specifically to the mother and her offspring. The prohibition reflects a reticence to kill two animals from the same family. In addition, it may reflect Israel's concern for lineage and the fear of exterminating a family line. Finally, if both the mother and her offspring are slaughtered on the same day, the result might be a confusion of the categories of life and death. Verses 29-30 specify that a sacrifice of thanksgiving must be eaten on the same day that it is sacrificed in order to be acceptable and effective.

Conclusion (vv. 31-33)

The conclusion opens with a call for obedience and the divine self-identification formula. The Israelites are warned not to profane the holy name of God (cf. 22:2) in order that God may be sanctified ("made holy") among the people. This suggests that the holiness of God is itself, at least in part, a construction of the community. Reference is made to God's saving activity in bringing Israel out of Egypt. The Exodus and the construction of holiness are both manifestations of the Yahweh-Israel relationship.

THE SACRED CALENDAR (CH. 23)

Leviticus 23 identifies the sacred times of the year and the rituals associated with them. The chapter imposes a temporal order on the Israelite year by marking out those times that are set apart for sacred activity and, by implication, those times that are not set apart for such activity. The social and theological construction of time, both in quantitative and qualitative terms, provides a context within which the Israelite community expresses and enacts its identity. The "temporal construct" provides a framework for community life by distinguishing various "kinds" of times: times that are *appropriate* for certain kinds of activities, times that *require* certain kinds of activities, and times that are *open* to various kinds of activities. The presence of multiple calendars in the Pentateuch indicates the importance of the "temporal" order for Israel (see Exod. 23:14-17; 34:18-26; Deut. 16:1-17; Lev. 23; Num. 28–29).

The temporal construction of order is significantly related to creation *and* history. Verse 2 speaks of the "set times" of Yahweh *(moʿadey yhwh)* that the Israelites are to observe. Genesis 1:14 indicates that one reason for the creation of the sun, moon, and stars is to mark out the sacred times *(moʿadim)* of the year. By observing and actualizing the holy nature of these set times, the Israelites participate in the ongoing construction and maintenance of the very good order of creation. Ritual is an act of creation (Gorman 1990, 215-27)! The Genesis text also indicates that history itself — "marking out days and years" — is part of the order of creation. Creation provides the context for both history and ritual, which are a significant expression and manifestation of the life of Israel.

Leviticus 23 divides the year into two parts by placing emphasis on the activities of the first month and the seventh month. The two-part division of the year reflects the two-part division of the day — day and night. Two seven-day observances are also required, one in the first month and one in the seventh month. In addition, seven holy convocations are identified in the calendar (vv. 7, 8, 21, 24, 27, 35, 36). The sabbath is excluded from this count in that it is a weekly rite and not a yearly, calendrical rite.

127

The weekly observance of the sabbath, however, is included in this list of sacred occasions.

Introductory Verses (vv. 1-2)

Verses 1-2 serve as a general introduction to the chapter and indicate that the instructions are provided for the whole community. The observance of these days is one means of experiencing community in terms of common and shared activities that bring and bind the people together in the context of the sacred.

The Sabbath (v. 3)

There are six days in which work is to be done, but the seventh day is a day of complete rest that requires a cessation of normal everyday work (cf. Gen. 2:2-3). The structure of the week provides a rhythm for life — days of work and a day of rest, common days and the holy day. The sabbath is part of the divinely created order of creation and is a ritual means of participating in, maintaining, and celebrating that order. The call to observe the sabbath is found in a number of texts: Exod. 20:8-11 (in the context of the Sinai covenant); Deut. 5:12-15 (in the context of the Exodus); Exod. 16:22-30 (cf. Num. 15:32-36; in the context of the wilderness). Thus, sabbath observance merges creation, history, and redemption.

Passover and Unleavened Bread (vv. 4-8)

Verse 4 is a restatement of v. 2. Verses 5-8 call for the observance of two distinct but related sacred times. At twilight on the fourteenth day of the first month, the Israelites are to offer the Passover sacrifice *(pesah)* to Yahweh. "At twilight," literally "between the two evenings," most probably refers to the sun's disappearance behind the horizon.

The fifteenth day begins a seven-day observance. This is the pilgrimage of unleavened bread, which became associated with the Passover. The first day of the unleavened pilgrimage (see Levine 1989, 156, 263-68) is a holy convocation. The people are not allowed to work at their normal occupations. For seven days they are to eat unleavened bread and offer offerings and sacrifices (Num. 28:16-25 specifies the types and quantity).

The Passover and unleavened bread are both associated elsewhere with the Exodus from Egypt (see especially Exod. 12). These observances became part of Israel's story about God's redemptive activity on its behalf. Passover and unleavened bread were ritual moments when the community could remember and actualize its story. When the children ask about the rituals, the response narrates what Yahweh did for "you." Yahweh's activity is to be an experienced reality for each generation (see Exod. 12:24-27). The ritual remembering of Yahweh's acts of redemption is a means of constructing community identity.

Firstfruits (vv. 9-14)

Verses 9-14 call for an offering of the first sheaf of the barley harvest, which took place early in the spring. The sheaf must be brought to the priest, who raises it in presentation to Yahweh on the day after the sabbath. This most likely refers to the first sabbath following the bringing of the sheaf to the priest. The reason for such a period of waiting is unclear. In addition, a burnt offering, a grain offering, and a drink offering must be presented. The offerer is not to eat any produce of the harvest until the presentation is completed.

The presentation of the first sheaf to Yahweh is a ritual enactment of thanksgiving that recognizes Yahweh's claim on the land and on the Israelites. It recognizes and celebrates the blessing of God experienced through a fertile earth. History and nature are merged in the ritual practices of Israel.

Firstfruits and Weeks (vv. 15-22)

Verses 15-21 call for the presentation of a grain offering of two loaves of bread made from choice flour and baked with leaven. This is the offering of firstfruits (*bikkurim;* cf. Exod. 22:29; 23:19; 34:26; Num. 18:12-13). Generally associated with the pilgrimage of weeks, this presentation is not named in Lev. 23 (cf. Exod.

129

34:22; Deut. 16:10; Exod. 23:16; Num. 28:26). It is dated by the offering of the sheaf of the barley harvest (see vv. 9-14): fifty days from the offering of the sheaf of the barley harvest, the wheat offering is to be offered in the form of two loaves. This is not termed a pilgrimage festival, and thus the Israelites are not required to go to the sanctuary. The language assumes, however, that they will do so ("you shall bring *from* your settlements" [v. 17]; "you shall *present*" [vv. 16, 18]; "the priest shall raise them" [v. 20], all suggest the sanctuary). It is possible, however, that a representative of the settlement would bring the offerings for the whole settlement. It is a holy convocation; no work is to be done (v. 21).

There are also a significant number of sacrifices and offerings presented to Yahweh at this time. Seven one-year-old lambs, a young bull, and two rams are presented as burnt offerings. The appropriate grain and drink offerings must be included. In addition, a goat is presented for a purification offering, and two one-year-old male lambs as a well-being offering.

This ritual constitutes the final observance of the first part of the year and, as such, marks the close of the first half of the year and the beginning of the second half. It may be that the additional sacrifices and offerings are required in order to effect passage from one part of the year to another. This suggests that the complete ritual process is more important than the meaning of any individual sacrifice.

Blowing the Trumpet (vv. 23-25)

Verses 23-25 state that the first day of the seventh month is to be a day of complete rest *(shabbaton)*. It is marked by the blowing of trumpets, a cessation of work, and the presentation of offerings to Yahweh. The observance of "weeks" closes one part of the year, while the blast of the trumpet and the day of rest opens the new.

The Day of Purification (vv. 26-32)

Verses 26-32 call for the observance of the day of purification on the tenth day of the seventh month (see Lev. 16). There are significant parallels between these verses and the summary verses of 16:29-34. No work is to be done *because* expiation/purification *(kipper)* is enacted on behalf of the Israelites. Harsh punishment is prescribed for the individual who does not fast (v. 29) or who does any work (v. 30). This day is to be observed from evening to evening (v. 32).

The Pilgrimage of Booths (vv. 33-36, 39-43)

Verses 33-36 call for the observance of the pilgrimage of booths. It begins on the fifteenth day of the seventh month and continues for seven days. The first day is a holy convocation and requires the cessation of work. Offerings are presented throughout the seven days. On the eighth day, there is another holy convocation, which requires the cessation of work and the presentation of sacrifices and offerings by fire. This festival concludes on the eighth day.

Verse 39 relates this festival to the gathering of the produce of the land, whereas v. 43 relates it to the Yahweh-Israel story, that is, the time of Israel's dwelling in "booths" when Yahweh brought them out of Egypt. This dual explanation provides clear evidence for the ongoing interpretive process within Israel as it sought to give new historical meaning to what were at one time primarily agricultural festivals. This interpretive process functions to weave together the fertility of the land and the national story. The separation of nature from history, with the accompanying belief that "true" Israelite faith was "historical," fails to account for the evidence in the texts. Israel recognized that its life on the land and its life as a redeemed community had significant theological connections. Yahweh is active in both nature and history!

Israel is to dwell in booths during the seven days of this observance (v. 42), which is to be characterized by joy (v. 40). It celebrates (a) the Exodus from Egypt, (b) the movement from slavery to freedom, and (c) the productivity of the land. It is a ritual enactment of deliverance from slavery to freedom. Ritual "remembering" provides an occasion to reconstruct, actualize, and concretize events from Israel's story. In ritual, Israel experiences again and again the passage to freedom. Ritual provides the context and the means for experiencing the redemptive activity of God.

Concluding Statement (vv. 37-38, 44)

Verses 37-38 and 44 conclude the chapter (vv. 39-40 disrupt the note) and provide a summary statement. Verse 44 states that Moses presented the instructions to the people. These instructions for the "sacred times" are a community concern. The appointed times structure the life of the people as they work their farms, tend to their animals, and live out their lives within the community. The sacred times construct a temporal order and provide a context for the life of the community.

THE LAMP, THE BREAD, AND BLASPHEMY (CH. 24)

The divine instructions in Lev. 24 are directed at the community (vv. 1-2a). There are three basic units: instructions for the lamp inside the tent (vv. 1-4; cf. Exod. 27:20-21); instructions for the bread placed inside the tent (vv. 5-9); and the story of a man who commits blasphemy and rulings on blasphemy and murder (vv. 10-23).

The precise reason for the inclusion of this material at just this point is not entirely clear. Leviticus 25, focusing on the Sabbatical and Jubilee Years, continues the discussion of the "sacred times" begun in ch. 23. Leviticus 24 is an intrusion. The lamp and the bread are related to the calendar in ch. 23 through a common identification of regularly prescribed activities. The reason for the location of the blasphemy case is uncertain.

The Lamp (vv. 1-4)

The instructions open with a call for the people to bring pure olive oil to burn in the lamp (v. 2b). Aaron is to place the lamp inside the outer room of the tent and insure that it burns regularly from evening to morning. This is a perpetual statute. While the phrase "the curtain of the covenant" refers to the curtain that separates the holy of holies from the outer room of the tent, it draws attention to the ark of the covenant that is behind the curtain and to the tablets of the covenant within it (see Exod. 25:21).

The text does not provide a rationale for the instructions concerning the lamp; there are three possibilities. (1) The lamp may constitute a reflection of the divine glory that dwells above the ark. (2) Since the lamp is located in relation to the curtain of the covenant, it may "image forth" the covenant relationship between Yahweh and Israel. (3) The fact that the lamp is to burn from evening to morning may indicate a connection with creation theology. The burning lamp provides ritual certainty of the coming of the day. It is, of course, possible that there is a purely pragmatic concern — it is a means of keeping light in the tent. The text does not provide a definitive answer.

The Bread (vv. 5-9)

Verses 5-9 provide instructions for the bread placed inside the tent. Elsewhere the priestly traditions refer to this bread as "the bread of the presence" (Exod. 25:30; 39:36). Twelve loaves, each made of two-tenths of an ephah of fine flour, are to be placed on a table in two rows, six to a row. Two-tenths of an ephah of flour would amount to approximately eight cups of flour, and thus the loaves are fairly large (Hartley 1992, 401; Rattray in Milgrom 1991, 890-901). The loaves are to be arranged every sabbath day, and they are to be eaten by the priests in a holy place. This bread is most holy. In addition, frankincense is to be provided for each row and functions as the representative portion to be burned on the altar (see the discussion of the grain offerings in Lev. 2). Thus, the loaves are understood as an offering to Yahweh.

This ruling reflects an older age when the bread was thought to be the food of the gods. Such views are not operative in the priestly traditions. The regular placing of the loaves before Yahweh is termed a "perpetual covenant" (this phrase appears elsewhere in the priestly traditions in Gen. 9:16; 17:7, 13, 18, 19; Exod. 31:16; Num. 18:19; 25:13). In that the bread comes "from the people of Israel" (v. 8), it may be associated with the perpetual nature of the Yahweh-Israel relationship. Terming these loaves "the bread of the presence" may indicate that the bread is a perpetual offering of the community to Yahweh, who turns to the community in looking upon and receiving the offering. The loaves are an indication of Yahweh's attentiveness to the covenant relationship.

A Case of Blasphemy (vv. 10-23)

Verses 10-23 open with a brief narrative of a man who commits an act of blasphemy. He has an Israelite mother from the tribe of Dan and an Egyptian father. The divine ruling that comes in response to his case gives rise to a series of instructions concerning blasphemy, murder, and the taking of animal life. The rulings are written in the form of two speeches (vv. 13-14, 15-22).

This man fought another man in the camp and in the process blasphemed the name of Yahweh (cf. vv. 15-16) in a curse (v. 11). He was brought to Moses and held in custody until an authoritative ruling could be obtained from Yahweh. Two specific aspects of the narrative should be noted. First, it is significant that the man is of mixed birth. It is this "mixed" status that calls for special inquiry in this case. Second, the fact that his mother is from the tribe of Dan may be significant (Levine 1989, 166). This tribe was associated with the sacred place constructed at Dan, which was considered non-Yahwistic by the Jerusalem religious establishment (see the narrative of Jeroboam's erection of a golden calf at Bethel and Dan in 1 Kings 12:25-33 and the negative evaluation of Jeroboam by the narrator in 1 Kings 13:33-34). This may reflect a subtle effort to construct a negative bias for the case.

In discussing the case, Lev. 24:11 uses two similar words. The man "cursed" or "stated clearly" *(nkb)* the name and "cursed" or "treated it lightly" *(qll)*. When taken together, these words mean that "he pronounced by cursing blasphemously" (Levine 1989, 166). He pointedly spoke the name without regard for its sanctity. Exodus 22:28 (Heb. v. 27) states, "You shall not curse *(teqallel)* God." Exodus 20:7 and Deut. 5:11 are formulated differently: "You shall not use ('lift up') the name of Yahweh your God in vain." The man charged with blasphemy pointedly spoke or cursed the name and took it lightly in a blasphemous way.

The fact that this case required Moses to seek a ruling from Yahweh demonstrates Israel's recognition that discovering the will of God is an ongoing process (Fishbane [1985, 98-106] notes three other examples in the Pentateuch: Num. 9:6-14; Num. 15:32-36; Num. 27:1-11). This process is both context specific and sensitive to new developments that might arise in community life and existence.

The divine ruling on the case of the blasphemer is found in v. 14. The people are to take the man "who cursed" (*hameqallel*) outside the camp. Those who heard the curse are to lay their hands on him, and the whole community is to stone him to death. The camp is the place of "life," and it must be protected from the contamination of a corpse. The laying on of hands is best understood as an act in which the witnesses who heard the blasphemy "hand over" the guilty party to the judgment of the community.

A series of pronouncements follow. The first (vv. 15-16) states that any person who curses (*yeqallel*) God must bear the sin of that act. In addition, anyone who specifically pronounces (*noqeb*) the name of Yahweh shall be put to death (*mot yumat*). The whole community must stone the guilty party. This ruling applies both to Israelites and to non-Israelites. The community is responsible to address violations of the social and religious order.

Verse 16b opens a unit that reflects a chiastic pattern (Wenham 1979, 312; Hartley 1992, 407): (A) one law for the visitor and the resident (v. 16b); (B) killing a human being (v. 17); (C) killing an animal (v. 18); (D) the law of equal retaliation or lex talionis (vv. 19-20); (C') killing an animal (21a); (B') killing a human being (21b); (A') one law for the visitor and the resident (v. 22). The structure places emphasis on the central statement, the law of retaliation: "an eye for an eye and a tooth for a tooth." It is not certain whether the statement is designed to "limit" violence — you may only take in retaliation what was lost — or to demand retribution — you must take what was taken from you. The contemporary reader may recognize that a call for retaliation ultimately functions to increase retaliatory acts of violence "without end." Thus, most prefer to see this as an attempt to limit violence. It must be remembered, however, that the priestly traditionists were concerned with creating a situation in which the guilty party was certain to bear the guilt associated with an action. Justice requires this. The law of retaliation, however, must be viewed within the context of the priestly affirmation of the value of life and the desire to preserve it. Context is crucial to theological reflection and construction.

These verses reflect a concern for two other issues: the killing of human beings and the killing of animals. The person who kills another must be put to death (vv. 17, 21b; cf. Gen. 9:5-6; Deut. 21:1-9). The form of the punishment *(mot yumat)* indicates that it is the responsibility of the community to execute the guilty party (see Milgrom 1970, 5-8).

A second concern in this chapter is the killing of animals. A clear distinction is made between the killing of an animal and the killing of a human being. One must pay compensation for the killing of an animal, which is clearly in this case livestock that belongs to another person (v. 21). With regard to livestock, the law of retaliation is better understood as a law of restitution: "and the one who kills an animal must pay a compensatory price for it, life for life" (v. 18).

Conclusion (v. 25)

Verse 25 concludes the chapter. It reports that Moses passed along the judgment and instructions of Yahweh to the people, and they took the blasphemer outside the camp and executed him by stoning. The chapter closes with the affirmation that the people did just as Yahweh had commanded Moses (cf. Num. 15:36 and 27:11).

SABBATICAL AND JUBILEE YEARS (CH. 25)

Leviticus 25 addresses several distinct but interrelated issues: instructions for the observance of the Sabbatical Year (vv. 1-7);

instructions for the observance of the Jubilee Year (vv. 8-17); problems and concerns that might arise in conjunction with the observance of the Jubilee Year (vv. 18-24); and issues related to the redemption of persons who have accumulated debt and/or become indentured workers (vv. 25-55).

Two primary statements regarding land and persons, both asserted by Yahweh, form the basis of these instructions. First, the land belongs to Yahweh and the Israelites dwell on it as tenants (vv. 23-24). Each Israelite has a right to a portion of the land. Because of this, the land may only be leased out, in order, for example, to pay a debt, but it is not to be sold without the owner maintaining the right of redemption. In the Jubilee Year, the land reverts to its primary holder. Second, the Israelites are the servants of Yahweh. Yahweh redeemed them from the land of Egypt (v. 55), and no Israelite may become the slave of another. This statement provides for the release of Israelites from indentured service.

The Sabbatical Year for the land and the Jubilee Year for land and persons have significant theological connections to other aspects of the priestly traditions. First, they are related to the weekly observance of the sabbath (see vv. 3-4). The relationship is made explicit in Exod. 23:10-13 (nonpriestly material). The Sabbatical Year, a year set apart to allow the land to rest, is an extension of the sabbath day, which is set apart as a day of rest (Gen. 2:2-3). Both the Sabbatical Year and the Jubilee Year (the date of which is determined by counting off "seven weeks of years," see Lev. 25:8) are related to the very good order of creation.

Second, the Sabbatical Year and the Jubilee Year reflect seven-day ritual processes (see the Introduction). Major ritual passage requires seven days: from chaos to order (Gen. 1:1–2:4a), from major impurity to purity (Lev. 14), from one status to another (Lev. 8–9). The Sabbatical and Jubilee Years are ritual times that shape both the life *of* the land and life *on* the land. They provide moments of restoration for persons and land.

The Sabbatical and Jubilee Year rulings are theologically important (see Ringe 1985, 16-32). They juxtapose images of Yahweh the creator and Yahweh the redeemer. They merge creation theology and a concern for social justice. In addition, they suggest an eschatological perspective that looks to a future day of redemption, rest, and release for persons and land alike. Ritual observance and social practice are intimately intertwined. Images of creation and redemption converge to construct equitable social practice.

The Sabbatical Year (vv. 1-7)

Verses 1-7 consist of divine instructions for the observance of the Sabbatical Year. This material is specifically associated with Mt. Sinai (cf. Lev. 25:1) and anticipates the time when Israel will dwell in the land (v. 2). Every seventh year is to be a sabbath of complete rest for the land, in which there is neither sowing nor pruning. Neither the produce that grows as a result of harvesting nor the aftergrowth of seeds that fall during the harvest are to be eaten. Whatever the land produces of itself, however, may be eaten by the household, the livestock, and the wild animals.

The Jubilee Year (vv. 8-17)

The Jubilee Year is determined by counting seven sabbaths of years (seven series of seven years), with the Jubilee Year being declared in the fiftieth year. The beginning of the Jubilee Year is marked by the blowing of the shophar horn on the day of purification (the tenth day of the seventh month; see 16:29; 23:27). The fiftieth year is to be "made holy," and liberty is to be proclaimed throughout the land. All persons shall return to their own land holdings.

The word "jubilee" is normally related to the word for "ram's horn" and is understood as the year in which the horn is blown and freedom granted. The priestly traditions view this as a community-wide enactment of release and freedom. The pragmatics of such an institution are, at best, difficult and complex, and the evidence for its practice is scant. Theologically, it remains an important aspect of the priestly *vision* of the Israelite community as the holy people of Yahweh.

The situation envisioned is not complex. Israelites who found themselves in economic straits for various reasons, for example, crop failure or livestock disease, would lease out their land holding, the *'ahuzzah* land, to another person, who would then use the land and possibly, at times, hold the original owners as indentured workers. In the Jubilee Year, land holdings returned to their original owners, and those who were indentured were set free.

Verses 13-17 caution against cheating and dishonesty in these transactions. Community life must be characterized by integrity in economic transactions. Payment was calculated on the basis of the number of years of use or harvests expected by the person leasing the land. Thus, if only a few years remained until the next Jubilee Year, the price would be lower.

Problems and Questions (vv. 18-24)

Verses 18-24 constitute a call for obedience with the promise of peace and prosperity. If the people are obedient, then the land will give its bounty and the people will be safe and satisfied (v. 19).

Verses 20-22 address a pragmatic question concerning the Sabbatical Year: What will the people eat in the seventh and eighth years (see vv. 11-12)? The crops of the sixth year will yield enough to provide food for three years, until a new crop can be harvested (cf. Exod. 16:22-26).

Verses 23-24 provide a bridge between units. They present the basic rationale for instructions regarding the land: it belongs to Yahweh. The Israelites do not own it; they hold it and tend it for Yahweh. Thus, a person's land holding may not be taken permanently from that person. These verses look back to the instructions in vv. 13-17 concerning the economics of land transactions and, at the same time, look forward to the instructions concerning redemption procedures for land.

Debts and Redemption (vv. 25-55)

Verses 25-55 detail various situations that might arise in regard to land and property debt and redemption procedures. Five basic situations are addressed (vv. 25-28; 29-34; 35-38; 39-46; 47-55).

Verses 25-28: The first statement provides the basic scenario. If a relative falls on difficult financial times and "sells" ("rents") a piece of land, there are three ways it may revert to the original holder. First, if possible, the next closest relative should redeem it (*go'alo;* v. 25). Second, if the original holder is able to "buy back" the land, the payment must reflect the time remaining before the Jubilee Year (v. 27). If the land is not redeemed by either of these methods, it reverts to the original holder at the Jubilee Year (v. 28).

Verses 29-34 address the issue of houses (vv. 29-31) and property that belongs to the Levites (vv. 32-34). If a person "sells" a dwelling that is within a walled city, it must be "redeemed" within a year, or it becomes the property of the person who purchased it (vv. 29-30). Houses in villages without walls may be redeemed at any time and must be returned to the original owner in the Jubilee Year (v. 31). The (agricultural) villages are more closely connected to the life of the land and are viewed as landed property.

Levitical houses located within levitical cities (see Num. 35:1-8) may be redeemed at any time. They must be released in the Jubilee Year (vv. 32-33). The land surrounding the levitical cities is the perpetual holding of the Levites and cannot be sold (v. 34). The levitical cities constitute part of the levitical benefits for their services.

Verses 35-38: If an Israelite experiences a difficult financial situation and becomes dependent on a relative, that person is to be treated as a resident non-Israelite (a *ger;* v. 35). Such a person must be allowed to work and must be paid accordingly. In addition, interest may not be charged, nor can a profit be made from her or him (vv. 36-37). Two motivational statements are attached to this ruling: "fear your God" and "remember God's redemptive activity for you when you were slaves." Ritual enactment and ethical enactment become one and the same thing in the priestly traditions. Both are means of locating oneself in relation to God, creation, and community.

Verses 39-46 address two related situations: (1) instructions on what happens if persons become so dependent that they have to sell themselves to an Israelite (vv. 39-43) and (2) instructions regarding non-Israelite slaves (vv. 44-46). Israelites who become dependent on another must remain as hired or bound laborers until the Jubilee Year, at which time they and their families must be released (vv. 39-41). A hired laborer works for wages, whereas a bound laborer works primarily to pay a debt. Israelites are not to become permanent slaves, nor are they to be treated harshly. The basis for the ruling is the Exodus (v. 42). Israelites may have permanent servants from the nations around them, and those servants may become the property of Israelites (vv. 44-46). A prohibition against the harsh treatment of these non-Israelite slaves is not included.

Verses 47-55: The situation now addressed deals with a non-Israelite buying an Israelite. It is the duty of the relatives to bring about the redemption of the person. Also, redemption may be obtained by the individual who has been sold (vv. 47-49). The price of redemption is calculated on the basis of the time before the next Jubilee Year, when the Israelite must be released, and also in terms of the time already worked. The Israelite is to be treated as a hired laborer under the authority of the non-Israelite. The non-Israelite, however, may not treat the Israelite harshly (the same word as in v. 43) in the sight of other Israelites. Should such harsh treatment be observed, steps must be taken to prevent it from happening again. The Israelite must be released in the Jubilee Year because the Israelites are the servants of Yahweh, who brought them out of Egypt (v. 55).

FAITHFUL WORSHIP OF YAHWEH (26:1-2)

Leviticus 26:1-2 consists of two statements that seem somewhat out of place in the present context. The first prohibits the production of idols, carved images, pillars, or figured stones (cf. Exod. 20:4-6). Making such objects indicates the intention to worship them. It is an affirmation of their existence. The second is a call to keep the sabbaths and to demonstrate a reverential attitude toward the sanctuary. Both prescriptions recognize the convergence of attitude *and* activity. The unit concludes with the divine self-identification formula: "I am Yahweh."

BLESSINGS AND CURSES (26:3-46)

Leviticus 26:3-46 states the blessings associated with obedience (vv. 3-13) and the curses associated with disobedience (vv. 14-39).

Even when curses, however, have brought Israel to the edge of annihilation, the people may still repent and find forgiveness (vv. 40-45). A final verse provides what, in all likelihood, functioned at one time as a concluding statement for the entire collection of instructions (v. 46).

A similar series of blessings and curses are found in Deut. 28 (cf. Exod. 23:22-33). Such series are known throughout the ancient Near East and are often associated with covenants (see Baltzer 1971; Hillers 1964; McCarthy 1963). The series in Deut. 28 is located in a covenant context, whereas Lev. 26 concludes the divine instructions for the community.

The blessings and the curses are presented as *images* to be seen as much as heard. It is important to "see" what is being said, or, to put this differently, it is important to envision the reality (of blessing or curse) that is constructed in, through, and by the words of the text.

The Blessings (vv. 3-13)

Verse 3 indicates that obedience leads to blessing and emphasizes the responsibility of the people. A list of the blessings follows. They may be grouped into four basic units that emphasize the activity of Yahweh (Hartley 1992, 457): agricultural bounty (vv. 4-5; "I will give"); success against enemies and peace in the land (vv. 6-8; "I will grant"); community fertility (vv. 9-10; "I will look"); and the presence of Yahweh in the midst of the community (vv. 11-12; "I will place"). Verse 13 relates the call to obedience to the Exodus from Egypt.

Agricultural Bounty (vv. 4-5)

Verse 4 specifies three aspects of Israel's agricultural life that will be affected by the blessing: the rains will come in their seasons, the land will yield its produce, and the trees will yield their fruit. Israelite agricultural life depended on the rains. Yahweh controls the rains, and, if the people are obedient, the rains will come and the land will be fertile and productive. The life of the community (obedience) is significantly related to the life of the land (productivity). The threshing of the grain will not be complete before it is time for the vines to be harvested (v. 5). The cycles of sowing and harvesting will begin to overlap. "Eating bread" is an image of well-being, security, prosperity, and satisfaction.

Success against Enemies (vv. 6-8)

Verse 6 presents an image of peace in the land; the people can live without fear. The two sources of fear that are specified are war and wild animals. This is an important window into the life of Israelites and their view of the world because it indicates that "fear" of the enemy and of wild animals was a very real part of their daily existence. War was a constant concern and source of fear for the Israelites. Obedience leads to peace.

Community Fertility (vv. 9-10)

Verse 9 provides two images of blessing. The first is the promise of fertility: Israel will be fruitful and multiply (cf. Gen. 1:28). The second focuses on the divine-human relationship: Yahweh will maintain the covenant with Israel. The present image of blessing, with its promise of fertility, is related to the covenant with the ancestors (Gen. 17). At the same time, the Sinai covenant is also in mind. The Sinai covenant is a central feature of the narrative traditions with which the priestly traditionists were working. The promise of blessing through obedience reflects the "conditional" nature of the Sinai covenant (see Exod. 19:3-6). Both promise and covenant provide theological background for blessing. Two additional images follow. The grain will not rot and the old will have to make way for the new. Fertility will abound, and the people will be satisfied.

The Presence of Yahweh (vv. 11-12)

If the people are obedient, Yahweh will dwell in their midst and neither loathe nor abhor them. Yahweh will actualize the statement, "I will be their God and they will be my people." This language echoes the divine covenant with Abraham in Gen. 17:7. Relationship is at the heart of covenant, and one way this is concretely realized is through Yahweh's presence in the midst of the Israelites (Exod. 25:8; 29:45-46). Yahweh's ongoing presence in the midst of Israel is a primary aspect of Israel's self-identity in the priestly traditions.

Verse 13 affirms that it was Yahweh who brought the people out of Egypt in order to release them from slavery. Redemption leads to obedience and obedience leads to blessing: productive land, peace, fertility, and the divine presence in the community. Obedience is one way in which Israel enacts and actualizes its identity.

The Curses (vv. 14-39)

Verses 14-39 list the curses that will follow if the Israelites are disobedient. The unit is introduced with a conditional clause, which provides an alternative choice for the people (vv. 14-15). Several curses mirror the blessings enumerated in vv. 3-13, although the curses are structured differently. Yahweh repeatedly gives Israel the opportunity to change its course of action and become obedient. Israel, however, repeatedly fails, and the power and intensity of the curses increase. The structure interweaves curses (vv. 16-17, 19-20, 22, 24-26) and threats of their intensification (vv. 18, 21, 23, 27). In each case, the intensification formula is followed by the divine statement, "I will . . ." (a similar pattern is found in Amos 4:6-11). Yahweh seeks to bring about a change in the behavior of the people. When this fails, Yahweh increases the intensity of the activity. The curses are Yahweh's response to the life of the community. Emphasis is repeatedly placed on the responsibility of the people to conduct themselves in appropriate ways. They must bear the consequences of their actions.

Verses 16-17 present two basic threats. First, terror and sickness will fall on the people. Second, Israel will plant seed to no avail because the enemy will eat it. The threat of attack is intensified by the statement, "I will set my face against you" (v. 17a; cf. v. 9). The threat operates within a larger set of images in which the turning of Yahweh's face toward a person or people indicates favor, blessing, or hope (see Exod. 33:11; Num. 6:25; Ps. 4:6 [Heb. 7]; 24:6; 27:8-9; 31:16 [Heb. 17]; 67:1 [Heb. 2]; 119:135). The threats of Israel's defeat counter the blessing of victory and security (vv. 7-8).

Verses 18-20: Because Israel has refused to obey, Yahweh will intensify the "curse" and punish Israel sevenfold because of its "sinful impurities" (v. 18). The association of "sevenfold" punishment with sins suggests that the punishment itself is now viewed as a ritual process, of sorts, in which Yahweh attempts to move the people from the status of sin to that of repentance and obedience. Curses are designed to punish sin and, at the same time, to turn Israel from its sin. The power of the nation will be broken, the waters will dry up (both the rains and the springs), and the strength of the people will come to nothing (v. 16). Neither the land nor the trees shall yield their produce (cf. the blessing in v. 4). The life of the people and the life of the land are interconnected.

Verses 21-22: The opening intensification formula in v. 21 reflects a slight shift: "I will continue to 'smite' you sevenfold for your sins." Wild beasts will be loosed upon the people (cf. v. 6) and they will take children and livestock. The people will die. The image of deserted roads shows a land reduced in population and empty of inhabitants.

Verses 23-26: The intensification formula now emphasizes that Yahweh will respond to Israel's hostility with hostility: "I will strike you, I myself, seven times because of your sinful impurities" (v. 24). The images used in vv. 25-26 suggest military attack and the agonies associated with a siege. Yahweh will bring the sword against Israel; the enemy will come in military strength; and it will execute vengeance for the covenant. The people have broken the covenant and justice must be executed! Withdrawal to the walled cities will be of no use. Pestilence will fall upon cities, and people will be given to the enemy. Bread will be scarce, and, even when it is eaten, it will not satisfy (cf. v. 5). Israel will experience the eruption of chaos, the breakdown of its life through military attack, the spread of disease, and a shortage of food.

Verses 27-33: The intensity increases as the threats move toward conclusion (note vv. 16, 18, 21, 24, 28). If the people continue to disobey and remain hostile, Yahweh will continue to be hostile with fury and will punish Israel seven times for its sins (vv. 27-28). The final series of images show the land destroyed, desolated, and empty of inhabitants. These are images of terror and despair.

"You shall consume the flesh of your children" (v. 29): This image is also found in Deut. 28:53 in the context of an attack and siege by an enemy. Lamentations 2:20-23 bewail the situation and give voice to the experience of its agony. The attack and siege of the enemy will leave the people hungry and drive them to extremes.

"The high places and the altars" (v. 30): The precise nature of these cultic places and objects is uncertain, although it is clear that they refer to pagan practices. The "high places" refer either to places of worship on hills and mountains or to raised structures built for worship. Israel's involvement in these pagan rituals will come to naught, and the high places will become mounds for their dead bodies. Yahweh will loathe Israel (cf. Jer. 14:19). The divine repulsion is a response to the sin of improper worship, as well as to the mounds of dead bodies.

"I will lay your cities waste" (v. 31-32): Images of waste, desolation, and destruction abound in these verses. Yahweh will make the cities a waste (cf. Isa. 5:5-6; 24:1-13; 49:19; Jer. 25:11, 18; 44:6, 22; Ezek. 5:14, and for similar images with different vocabulary, cf. Isa. 6:11-12; Jer. 4:19-28). In addition, the "sanctuaries" will be desolate (v. 31). The plural indicates that this refers to the multiple places of worship used by the people and not to the sanctuary of Yahweh. The sacrifices that provide "a pleasing fragrance" (e.g., the burnt offering, the grain offering, and the well-being offering) will not be accepted because the Yahweh-Israel relationship is broken. The enemies that come to settle in the land will be appalled by the waste and desolation found in it.

"I will scatter you" (v. 33): This verse leads to the final and ultimate act of punishment and fury — exile from the land. The relationship between the people and the land will be broken because the relationship between the people and Yahweh is broken. Exile is loss of everything — land, promises, cult, home, and political power. The book of Lamentations consists of laments over Jerusalem's fall to Babylon in the sixth century B.C.E.. It gives voice to the despair that accompanied that moment in Israel's history: "How it remains empty, the city once filled with people!" (Lam. 1:1; cf. Psalm 137).

The Land and Exile (vv. 34-39): These verses discuss two issues relating to exile. First, the land will enjoy its sabbaths while the people are in exile (see Lev. 25). Second, the people who go into exile, those who survive the attack and siege, will live in terror, in constant fear of violence, and in a constant state of powerlessness. They will perish in exile and waste away because of their sins and the sins of their ancestors. Exile threatens the destruction and end of the community.

Hope in the Midst of Exile (vv. 40-46)

Verses 40-45 present a change in tone and viewpoint. They indicate that destruction need not be the final image. Hope remains! The movement from destruction and despair to hope reflects the dynamic interaction of Yahweh and Israel. If Israel will confess its iniquity, demonstrate humility, and make amends, then Yahweh will remember the covenant made with the ancestors. Even in the midst of waste, devastation, and exile, the ancient promise of Yahweh remains an active possibility in the life of Israel. ·

Yahweh will not completely destroy the nation. That would constitute a breaking of the covenant. God's "remembering" of the covenant made when the Israelites came out of Egypt overrides the punishment. The people, however, remain responsible for their actions. The blend of divine grace and human responsibility is apparent. This is a both/and situation precisely because it is viewed in relational terms. Both parties must respond and act.

Conclusion (v. 46)

Verse 46 closes the chapter. It locates the divine speeches on Mt. Sinai. A similar reference is found in Lev. 7:38 in what acts as a concluding statement for the collection of instructions regarding the sacrifices and offerings. The reference to Sinai is also found in 27:34 in the final verse of the book. Finally, ch. 25 opens with a statement that Yahweh spoke to Moses on Mt. Sinai (v. 1). It may be that 26:46 initially acted as a conclusion to a small, independent collection of instructions (chs. 25–26). This would account for the mutual discussion of the sabbatical rest of the land in ch. 25 and 26:34. Leviticus 26:46, however, appears to refer to more than that small collection. Initially it may have functioned as the closing statement for the holiness code. It is possible that, at one time, it functioned as a concluding statement for the book of Leviticus. If so, ch. 27 would obviously be a later addition.

ECONOMICS OF THE SANCTUARY

Leviticus 27:1-34

Leviticus 27 seems out of place following the list of blessings and curses in ch. 26. It addresses issues relating to the payment of vows and the dedication of various persons, animals, and objects. A close relationship exists between "religion" and "economics," and the priesthood played a central role in establishing economic values.

PAYMENT OF VOWS (VV. 1-8)

The first situation deals with a vow that requires the equivalent of a human being for payment and identifies the amount of silver required to "redeem" such a vow. For example, Hannah asks for a child and vows to dedicate the child to the service of the sanctuary at Shiloh (1 Sam. 1:10-11). Jephthah vows to sacrifice the first person to come out of his house if he should be victorious in battle. Unfortunately, when his daughter came out to meet him, he chose to perform the sacrifice rather than pay the price of redemption (Judges 11:29-40).

The equivalent amounts are assigned on the basis of gender and age and calculated in terms of silver shekels, using the sanctuary shekel as a standard.

	Male	*Female*
Over 60 years of age:	15	10
20-60 years of age:	50	30
5-20 years of age:	20	10
1 month to 5 years of age:	5	3

The values are based on labor productivity, although the types of labor considered of value are not specified. The list suggests that menial and heavy labor are in mind because a higher value is assigned to younger persons and to males. These evaluations are extremely high, and it is difficult to imagine that such payments were often made. Indeed, v. 8 makes it possible for people to be assessed according to their economic ability (on "redemption" of the firstborn, see Num. 18:15-18).

ANIMALS THAT ARE VOWED (Vv. 9-13)

If a clean animal has been vowed, that specific animal must be offered. Dedication makes the animal holy, and a substitute, good or bad, cannot be offered. If a substitution is made, the owner must forfeit both animals. If the animal is unclean, it must be brought to the priest, who will assess its value. In addition to the payment of its assessed value, an additional one-fifth of its value must be paid.

A DEDICATED HOUSE (Vv. 14-15)

If a house is consecrated to Yahweh, the priest will assess its value, a non-negotiable assessment, and the owner may redeem it through payment of the assessed value plus an additional one-fifth.

THE DEDICATION OF LAND AND PROPERTY (Vv. 16-21)

Verses 16-19 deal with the assessment of inherited land (*'ahuzzah* land; cf. ch. 25). Its assessment is based on the quantity of seed it takes to sow the field; fifty shekels of silver is required for every homer of barley seed. A "homer" is a measurement associated with, in this case, the amount of seed an ass could carry (Levine 1989, 196). If the field is consecrated in the Jubilee Year, the assessment stands. If it is consecrated prior to the Jubilee Year, then the value is reduced in terms of the number of years the land may be worked before it reverts to the original owner. If the original owner chooses to redeem the land, the cost is the assessed value plus an additional one-fifth. If the owner does not redeem the land or sells it to another, it is no longer redeemable. In the Jubilee Year, it becomes holy to Yahweh and is termed a "devoted" *(herem)* field. At that time it becomes the property of the priests.

It is not entirely clear what "sell" means in v. 20. The issue is complicated by the uncertain meaning of the phrase "a field of *herem*" (v. 21). *Herem* means "dedicated to Yahweh" (see, for example, the story of Achan in Josh. 7). At present, the interpretation is that a field that is neither redeemed nor sold becomes dedicated to Yahweh in the Jubilee Year.

Purchased Land (Vv. 22-25)

Verses 22-25 deal with the purchase of consecrated land that is not part of a family holding. The priest assesses the value in relation to the Jubilee Year; the price must be paid on that day. It is a sacred donation to Yahweh. Thus, if a person had paid to lease a piece of land (see ch. 25) and then consecrated it to Yahweh, the assessed value must be paid on the day of assessment. Verse 25 indicates that all assessments are made in terms of the sanctuary shekel, which is computed as twenty grains per shekel.

Miscellaneous Rules for Dedication (Vv. 26-33)

Verses 26-33 address a variety of issues. The firstborn of animals may not be consecrated (i.e., dedicated) to Yahweh because they already belong to Yahweh (vv. 26-27; see Num. 18:15-18). If it is an unclean animal, an animal that cannot be placed on the altar, it may be ransomed by payment of its assessed value plus one-fifth. If it is not redeemed, it is sold for its assessed value.

Nothing that has been devoted to Yahweh for destruction may be redeemed. Any object or person that is devoted *(herem)* is most holy to Yahweh. The statement referring to human beings who have been dedicated to Yahweh recalls the ruling of Exod. 22:20 [Heb. 22:19] that no redemption price is available for one who has sacrificed to other gods.

Verses 30-33 address the issue of tithes from the land (vv. 30-31) and tithes from the herd and flock (vv. 32-33). Tithes may be redeemed by paying the assessed value plus one-fifth. In terms of animals, the tenth animal is holy and belongs to Yahweh. There can be no substitution. If a substitution is made, then both animals are holy and neither may be redeemed.

CONCLUDING STATEMENT (V. 34)

The book closes with the statement: "These are the commandments that Yahweh commanded Moses to give to the people of Israel on Mt. Sinai." This concludes the initial giving of instructions at the mountain. Further instructions and rulings will be given before the Israelites depart from the mountain on their way to the land (the departure is noted in Num. 10:11). Thus, the structure of the larger story recognizes the open-ended nature of divine instruction in response to new situations and questions in the community.

BIBLIOGRAPHY

Anderson, G. A.
1992   "Sacrifice and Sacrificial Offerings, OT." Pp. 870-86 in
         The Anchor Bible Dictionary, vol. 5. New York: Dou-
         bleday.

Baltzer, K.
1971   *The Covenant Formulary in the Old Testament, Jewish and
         Early Christian Writings.* Trans. D. E. Green. Philadel-
         phia: Fortress Press.

Bell, C. M.
1992   *Ritual Theory, Ritual Practice.* New York and Oxford:
         Oxford University Press.

Bigger, S. F.
1979   "The Family Laws of Leviticus 18 in Their Setting."
         Journal of Biblical Literature 98:187-203.

Blenkinsopp, J.
1976   "The Structure of P." *Catholic Biblical Quarterly* 38:275-
         92.

Brueggemann, W.
1995   *The Psalms and the Life of Faith.* Ed. P. D. Miller. Min-
         neapolis: Fortress.

Carmichael, C. M.
1982   "Forbidden Mixtures." *Vetus Testamentum* 32:394-415.

Carroll, M. P.
1985   "One More Time: Leviticus Revisited." Pp. 117-26 in *Anthropological Approaches to the Old Testament*. Ed. B. Lang. Issues in Religion and Theology 8. London: SPCK; Philadelphia: Fortress.

Cohn, R. L.
1981   *The Shape of Sacred Space: Four Biblical Studies.* American Academy of Religion Studies in Religion 23. Chico, Calif.: Scholars Press.

Davies, D.
1977   "An Interpretation of Sacrifice in Leviticus." *Zeitschrift für die alttestamentliche Wissenschaft* 89:387-98.

Day, J.
1989   *Molech: A God of Human Sacrifice in the Old Testament.* Cambridge: Cambridge University Press.

Douglas, M.
1979   *Purity and Danger: An Analysis of the Concepts of Pollution and Taboo.* 1966. Reprint, London and Boston: Routledge & Kegan Paul.

Dozeman, T. B.
1989   *God on the Mountain: A Study of Redaction, Theology and Canon in Exodus 19–24.* Society of Biblical Literature Monograph Series 37. Atlanta: Scholars Press.

Eilberg-Schwartz, H.
1990   *The Savage in Judaism: An Anthropology of Israelite Religion and Ancient Judaism.* Bloomington and Indianapolis: Indiana University Press.

Elliger, K.
1966   *Leviticus.* Handbuch zum Alten Testament 4. Tübingen: J. C. B. Mohr (Paul Siebeck).

Feldman, E.

1977   *Biblical and Post-Biblical Defilement and Mourning: Law as Theology.* The Library of Jewish Laws and Ethics. New York: Yeshiva University Press, KTAV.

Firmage, E.

1990   "The Biblical Dietary Laws and the Concept of Holiness." Pp. 177-208 in *Studies in the Pentateuch.* Ed. J. A. Emerton. Vetus Testamentum Supplements 41. Leiden: Brill.

Fishbane, M.

1979   *Text and Texture: Close Readings of Selected Biblical Texts.* New York: Schocken.

1985   *Biblical Interpretation in Ancient Israel.* Oxford: Clarendon; New York: Oxford University Press.

Fretheim, T. E.

1991   *Exodus.* Interpretation. Louisville: John Knox.

Frymer-Kensky, T.

1983   "Pollution, Purification, and Purgation in Biblical Israel." Pp. 399-414 in *The Word of the Lord Shall Go Forth: Essays in Honor of David Noel Freedman in Celebration of His Sixtieth Birthday.* Ed. C. L. Meyers and M. O'Connor. Winona Lake, Ind.: Eisenbrauns.

1989   "Law and Philosophy: The Case of Sex in the Bible." *Semeia* 45:89-102.

Gorman, Jr. F. H.

1990   *The Ideology of Ritual: Space, Time and Status in the Priestly Theology.* Journal for the Study of the Old Testament, Supplement Series 91. Sheffield: JSOT Press.

1993   "Priestly Rituals of Founding: Time, Space, and Status." Pp. 47-64 in *History and Interpretation: Essays in Honour of John H. Hayes.* Ed. M. P. Graham, W. P. Brown, and J. K. Kuan. Journal for the Study of the Old Testament, Supplement Series 173. Sheffield: JSOT Press.

1994   "Ritual Studies and Biblical Studies: Assessment of the Past, Prospects for the Future." *Semeia* 67:13-36.

Grimes, R. L.
1992   "Reinventing Ritual." *Soundings* 75:21-41.

Grosz, E.
1993   "Bodies and Knowledge: Feminism and the Crisis of Reason." Pp. 187-215 in *Feminist Epistemologies*. Ed. L. Alcoff and E. Potter. New York and London: Routledge.

Gruber, M. I.
1987   "Women in the Cult According to the Priestly Code." Pp. 35-48 in *Judaic Perspectives on Ancient Israel*. Ed. J. Neusner et al. Philadelphia: Fortress.

Haran, M.
1961   "The Complex of Ritual Acts Performed Inside the Tabernacle." *Scripta Hierosolymitana* 8:272-302.
1978   *Temples and Temple-Service in Ancient Israel: An Inquiry into the Character of Cult Phenomena and the Historical Setting of the Priestly School*. Oxford: Clarendon.

Hartley, J. E.
1992   *Leviticus*. Word Bible Commentary 4. Dallas: Word.

Heider, G. C.
1985   *The Cult of Molek: A Reassessment*. Journal for the Study of the Old Testament, Supplement Series 43. Sheffield: JSOT Press.

Hillers, D. R.
1964   *Treaty-Curses and the Old Testament Prophets*. Biblica et orientalia 16. Rome: Pontifical Biblical Institute.

Horton, Jr. F. L.
1973   "Form and Structure in Laws Relating to Women: Leviticus 18:6-18." Pp. 20-33 in *The Society of Biblical Literature Seminar Papers, 1973,* vol. 1. Chico, Calif.: Scholars Press.

Houston, W.
1993   *Purity and Monotheism: Clean and Unclean Animals in Biblical Law.* Journal for the Study of the Old Testament, Supplement Series 140. Sheffield: JSOT Press.

Houten, C. van.
1991   *The Alien in Israelite Law.* Journal for the Study of the Old Testament, Supplement Series 107. Sheffield: JSOT Press.

Hyers, C.
1984   *The Meaning of Creation: Genesis and Modern Science.* Atlanta: John Knox.

Jay, N.
1985   "Sacrifice as Remedy for Having Been Born of Woman." Pp. 283-309 in *Immaculate and Powerful: The Female in Sacred Image and Social Reality.* Ed. C. W. Atkinson et al. Boston: Beacon.

Jennings, T. W.
1982   "On Ritual Knowledge." *Journal of Religion* 62:111-27.

Jenson, P. P.
1992   *Graded Holiness: A Key to the Priestly Conception of the World.* Journal for the Study of the Old Testament, Supplement Series 106. Sheffield: JSOT Press.

Kearney, P. J.
1977   "Creation and Liturgy: The P Redaction of Ex 25–40." *Zeitschrift für die alttestamentliche Wissenschaft* 89:375-87.

Kiuchi, N.

1987   *The Purification Offering in the Priestly Literature: Its Meaning and Function.* Journal for the Study of the Old Testament, Supplement Series 56. Sheffield: JSOT Press.

Knight, G. A. F.

1981   *Leviticus.* Edinburgh: Saint Andrews; Philadelphia: Westminster.

Knohl, I.

1987   "The Priestly Torah Versus the Holiness School: Sabbath and the Festivals." *Hebrew Union College Annual* 58:65-117.

1995   *The Sanctuary of Silence: The Priestly Torah and the Holiness School.* Minneapolis: Fortress.

Levenson, J. D.

1988   *Creation and the Persistence of Evil: The Jewish Drama of Divine Omnipotence.* San Francisco: Harper & Row.

Levine, B.

1965   "The Descriptive Tabernacle Texts of the Pentateuch." *Journal of the American Oriental Society* 85:307-18.

1974   *In the Presence of the Lord: A Study of Cult and Some Cultic Terms in Ancient Israel.* Studies in Judaism in Late Antiquity 5. Leiden: Brill.

1989   *Leviticus.* Jewish Publication Society Torah Commentary. Philadelphia: Jewish Publication Society.

Lohfink, N.

1982   "Creation and Salvation in Priestly Theology." *Theology Digest* 30:3-6.

Mann, T. W.

1971   "The Pillar of Cloud in the Reed Sea Narrative." *Journal of Biblical Literature* 90:15-30.

McCarthy, D. J.

1978   *Treaty and Covenant: A Study in the Ancient Oriental Documents and in the Old Testament.* Analecta Biblica 21. Rome: Pontifical Biblical Institute.

Milgrom, J.

1967   "The Cultic *Šĕgāgâ* and Its Influence in Psalms and Job." *Jewish Quarterly Review* 58:73-79.

1970   *Studies in Levitical Terminology, I. The Encroacher and the Levite. The Term 'Aboda.* Berkeley, Los Angeles, and London: University of California Press.

1971   "A Prolegomenon to Lev. 17:11." *Journal of Biblical Literature* 90:149-56.

1976a   *Cult and Conscience: The ASHAM and the Priestly Doctrine of Repentance.* Studies in Judaism in Late Antiquity 18. Leiden: Brill.

1976b   "Sacrifices and Offerings, OT." Pp. 763-71 in *The Interpreter's Dictionary of the Bible,* Supplementary Volume. Nashville: Abingdon.

1977   "The Betrothed Slave-Girl, Leviticus 19:20-22." *Zeitschrift für die alttestamentliche Wissenschaft* 89:43-49.

1981   "Vertical Retribution: Ruminations on *Parashat* and *Shelah.*" *Conservative Judaism* 34:11-16.

1983   *Studies in Cultic Theology and Terminology.* Studies in Judaism in Late Antiquity 36. Leiden: Brill.

1990   *Numbers.* Jewish Publication Society Torah Commentary. Philadelphia: Jewish Publication Society.

1991   *Leviticus 1–16.* The Anchor Bible 3. New York: Doubleday.

Nelson, R. D.

1993   *Raising Up a Faithful Priest: Community and Priesthood in Biblical Theology.* Louisville: Westminster/John Knox.

Newing, E. G.

1981   "A Rhetorical and Theological Analysis of the Hexateuch." *South East Asia Journal of Theology* 22:1-15.

1985   "The Rhetoric of Hope: The Theological Structure of Genesis–2 Kings." *Colloquium* 17:1-15.

Noth, M.
1965   *Leviticus: A Commentary.* Rev. ed. Philadelphia: Westminster.

Péter, R.
1977   "L'imposition des mains dans l'Ancien Testament." *Vetus Testamentum* 27:48-55.

Pilch, J. J.
1981   "Biblical Leprosy and Body Symbolism." *Biblical Theology Bulletin* 11:108-13.

Plaskow, J.
1990   *Standing Again at Sinai: Judaism from a Feminist Perspective.* San Francisco: Harper & Row.

Rainey, A. F.
1970   "The Order of Sacrifices in Old Testament Ritual Texts." *Biblica* 51:485-98.

Rattray, S.
1987   "Marriage Rules, Kinship Terms and Family Structure in the Bible." Pp. 537-44 in *The Society of Biblical Literature Seminar Papers, 1987.* Atlanta: Scholars Press.
1991   "The Biblical Measures of Capacity." Pp. 890-901 in *Leviticus 1–16.* The Anchor Bible 3. J. Milgrom. New York: Doubleday.

Rendtorff, R.
1985   *Leviticus.* Biblischer Kommentar: Altes Testament 3/1. Neukirchen-Vluyn: Neukirchener Verlag.
1989   " 'Covenant' as a Structuring Concept in Genesis and Exodus." *Journal of Biblical Literature* 108:385-93.

Ringe, S. H.

1985   *Jesus, Liberation, and the Biblical Jubilee: Images for Ethics and Christology.* Overtures to Biblical Theology 19. Philadelphia: Fortress.

Sanders, J. A.

1972   *Torah and Canon.* Philadelphia: Fortress.

1987   *From Sacred Story to Sacred Text: Canon as Paradigm.* Philadelphia: Fortress.

Schwartz, B. J.

1986   "A Literary Study of the Slave-girl Pericope — Leviticus 19:20-22." *Scripta Hierosolymitana* 31:241-55.

1991   "The Prohibitions Concerning the 'Eating' of Blood in Leviticus 17." Pp. 34-66 in *Priesthood and Cult in Ancient Israel.* Ed. G. A. Anderson and S. M. Olyan. Journal for the Study of the Old Testament, Supplement Series 125. Sheffield: JSOT Press.

Snaith, N. H.

1977   *Leviticus and Numbers.* New Century Bible. London: Oliphants.

Soler, J.

1979   "The Dietary Prohibitions of the Hebrews." *New York Review of Books* 26:24-30.

Speiser, E. A.

1960   "Leviticus and the Critics." Pp. 29-45 in *Yehezkel Kaufmann Jubilee Volume.* Ed. M. Haran. Jerusalem: Magnes.

Tawil, H.

1980   "'Azazel the Prince of the Steepe: A Comparative Study." *Zeitschrift für die alttestamentliche Wissenschaft* 92:43-59.

Thompson, L. L.

1981 "The Jordan Crossing: Sidqot Yahweh and World Building." *Journal of Biblical Literature* 100:343-58.

Vriezen, Th. C.

1950 "The Term *hizza:* Lustration and Consecration." *Oudtestamentische Studiën* 7:201-35.

Wenham, G. J.

1979 *The Book of Leviticus.* New International Commentary on the Old Testament. Grand Rapids, Mich.: Eerdmans.

1983 "Why Does Sexual Intercourse Defile (Lev 15.18)?" *Zeitschrift für die alttestamentliche Wissenschaft* 95:432-34.

Whitekettle, R.

1991 "Leviticus 15.18 Reconsidered: Chiasm, Spatial Structure and the Body." *Journal for the Study of the Old Testament* 49:31-45.

Wold, D. J.

1979 "The KARETH Penalty in P: Rationale and Cases." Pp. 1-25 in *The Society of Biblical Literature Seminar Papers 1979,* vol. 1. Chico, Calif.: Scholars Press.

Wright, C. J. H.

1984 "What Happened Every Seven Years in Israel? Old Testament Sabbatical Institutions for Land, Debts and Slaves." *Evangelical Quarterly* 56:129-38, 193-201.

1992 "Sabbatical Year." Pp. 857-61 in *The Anchor Bible Dictionary,* vol. 5. New York: Doubleday.

Wright, D. P.

1991 "The Spectrum of Priestly Impurity." Pp. 150-81 in *Priesthood and Cult in Ancient Israel.* Ed. G. A. Anderson and S. M. Olyan. Journal for the Study of the Old Testament, Supplement Series 125. Sheffield: JSOT Press.

Wright, D. P. and R. N. Jones
1992   "Leprosy." Pp. 277-82 in *The Anchor Bible Dictionary,* vol. 4. New York: Doubleday.